PART ONE
FASHION DESIGN

Felicity Everett
Consultant: Howard Tangye

(fashion designer, illustrator and teacher of
fashion illustration at St Martin's School of Art,
London)

Edited by Janet Cook

Designed by Camilla Luff

Cover design by Nerissa Davies

Illustrated by Nicky Dupays, Howard Tangye, Chris Lyon, Lynne Riding,
Lynne Robinson, Terry Beard, Susan Alcantarilla, Lisa Darnell,
Kathy James and Peter Bull.

Commissioned photography by Geoff Brightling

Picture research by Constance Novis

Contents

About fashion

Fashion is fun, colourful and glamorous. For those involved in the fashion industry, it is also very hard work. Part one of this book takes a look at fashion from every angle. It explores the flamboyant show-business aspect of the industry – the big names, the fashion shows and the international fashion capitals. It also takes you behind the scenes, into the organized chaos of a fashion studio, to see how clothes are designed, made and sold.

In the latter half of part one there is a practical guide to fashion illustration, covering a wide variety of artist's techniques. It provides a basis for anyone envisaging a career in fashion illustration, and is also ideal for those wanting to take it up as a hobby.

Where they first appear in a section, technical terms are printed in **bold italics** and explained in the glossary on page 64. The end of part one is packed with useful reference material on books, courses and careers in fashion design, illustration and other fashion-related fields.

What is fashion design?

Many people sketch clothes for fun, without considering whether they could actually be made. Professional fashion designers have to be more practical. *Their* design sketches have to work as patterns, and then as finished garments. No matter how good a design looks on paper, it is no use if it is impractical to make or wear.

What makes a good designer?

To be a good fashion designer, you do not necessarily have to be good at drawing. Some designers don't sketch at all, they just work with fabric. However, you do need imagination and a practical knowledge of how clothes are made. Having the ability to make your own clothes can be a great advantage.

Design competitions

Many colleges enter students for design competitions, sponsored by clothing or fabric companies. This gives the students commercial experience, and provides fresh talent for the companies. Below are two award-winning knitwear designs from the **Courtelle Design Awards.**

Becoming a fashion designer

College prospectuses

If you want to become a professional fashion designer, the best way is to study fashion design at college. As well as teaching you about the technical and artistic side of the subject, some courses include a year working in the fashion industry, to give students a taste of commercial fashion design. Others offer the chance to visit *fashion houses* abroad. You can find out more about some of the courses available on pages 62-63.

Men's knitwear designs for **Burton** with knitted samples attached.

Designer Alison Carter of Brighton Polytechnic with the finished sweaters.

Different types of fashion design

Haute couture

The type of design which predominated until the 1950s was **haute couture** (French for fine tailoring). A couture garment is made for an individual customer. Look and fit take priority over the cost of materials and the time it takes to make.

CHANEL

Mass market

These days the fashion industry relies more on the **mass market**. This caters for a wide range of customers, producing **ready-to-wear** clothes in large quantities and standard sizes. Cheap materials, creatively used, produce affordable high street fashion.

benetton

Designer label

Designer label clothes are a cross between **couture** and **mass market**. They are not made for individual customers, but great care is taken in the choice and cut of the fabric. Clothes are made in small quantities to guarantee exclusivity, so they are quite costly.

LACOSTE

Areas of work

There are three main ways in which designers can work.

1. Working freelance

Freelance designers work for themselves. They sell their work to *fashion houses*, direct to shops or to clothing manufacturers. The garments bear the *buyer's** label.

2. Working in-house

In-house designers are employed full-time by one fashion company. Their designs are the property of that company, and cannot be sold to anyone else.

3. Setting up a company

Fashion designers sometimes set up their own companies. Many people find this more satisfying than working for someone else, as their designs are sold under their own label.

On pages 10-13 you can find out more about how fashion designers work.

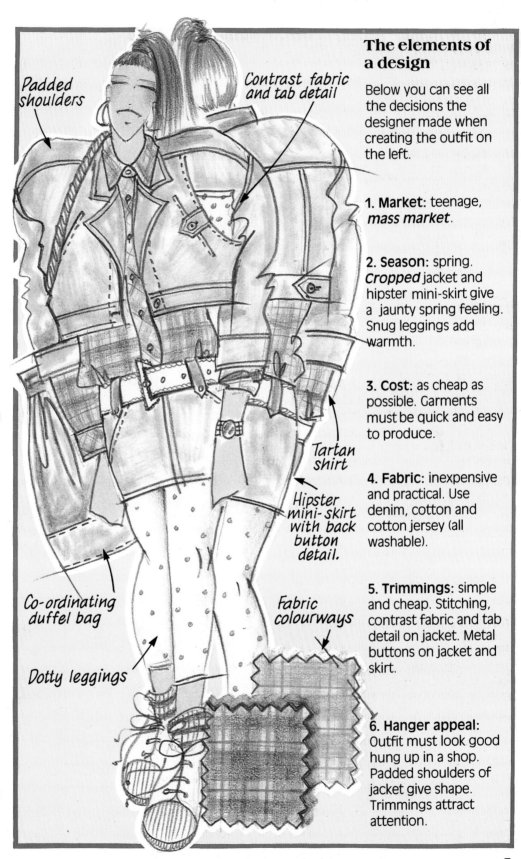

Padded shoulders

Contrast fabric and tab detail

Tartan shirt

Hipster mini-skirt with back button detail.

Co-ordinating duffel bag

Fabric colourways

Dotty leggings

The elements of a design

Below you can see all the decisions the designer made when creating the outfit on the left.

1. Market: teenage, *mass market*.

2. Season: spring. *Cropped* jacket and hipster mini-skirt give a jaunty spring feeling. Snug leggings add warmth.

3. Cost: as cheap as possible. Garments must be quick and easy to produce.

4. Fabric: inexpensive and practical. Use denim, cotton and cotton jersey (all washable).

5. Trimmings: simple and cheap. Stitching, contrast fabric and tab detail on jacket. Metal buttons on jacket and skirt.

6. Hanger appeal: Outfit must look good hung up in a shop. Padded shoulders of jacket give shape. Trimmings attract attention.

* You can find out more about buyers on page 13.

Twentieth century fashions

"New" fashions are hardly ever completely original. They are very often new versions of styles which have been fashionable in the past. Although fashion changes year by year, major developments are easier to detect once a particular era has passed.

It is useful for designers to study the history of fashion, as it provides a context for their work and a source of ideas. On the next four pages you can see the major developments within the world of fashion during the twentieth century.

The Edwardian era

The grandeur and extravagance of the Edwardian era (1890-1910) were reflected in the fashions of the time. For example, women's dresses were long and full-skirted and they often had *bustles*, which emphasized the hips. Styles like this used vast quantities of sumptuous fabrics such as silk, satin and *crêpe de chine*. Edwardian men wore *frock coats*, so-called because of their flared, skirt-like shape, and top hats for formal occasions.

1910

The Russian ballet peformed **Scheherezade** in Paris in 1910, in which dancers wore flowing Eastern costumes. This started a fashion for softly draped, oriental-style dresses which changed the shape of women's fashion.

The Great War

Changes in dress during World War I were dictated more by necessity than fashion. Many men wore uniform. Women wore hardwearing, practical clothes, because they took over jobs previously done by men. These conditions influenced fashion after the war.

1920s

The roles women had adopted during the war gave them the confidence to dress more boldly in the 20s.
A *couturier* called **Coco Chanel*** popularized chic, mannish styles in new fabrics, like jersey. Women wore their skirts shorter than before.

Chanel suit from 1926

Oxford bags were a popular men's fashion of the 20s. These were baggy trousers, about 16" wide at the ankles, which were first worn by students at Oxford University, England. They were revived as a women's fashion in the 30s and for women and men in the 70s.

The Bystander, 1925

* You can find out more about **Chanel** on page 24.

The bias cut

In the late 20s and early 30s, a French *couturier*, **Madeleine Vionnet** made a great technical advance in *haute couture.* She began to cut cloth on the "bias" (or diagonally, across the fabric's lengthwise threads). Her dresses therefore clung flatteringly to the body's curves.

1930s

Women's fashions in the 30s moved away from the brash, daring styles of the 20s towards a more romantic, feminine silhouette. Hemlines dropped. Backless evening gowns and soft, slim-fitting day dresses became popular. Men's clothes continued the informal, practical trend that had dominated since the end of World War I. Raincoats with military-style *epaulettes*, and *trilby hats* were popular outdoor garments of the 30s.

1940s

The Depression of the 30s was followed by the Second World War in 1939. Wartime again took its toll on fashion. Clothes became practical and hardwearing once more as women went back to work in factories and on farms, while the men were away fighting. The war brought shortages, making rationing of most goods necessary. This affected the cut and style of clothes.

The rationing of cloth meant that women's dresses and skirts became closer fitting and hemlines rose to knee-length, to save fabric. Civilian styles imitated the smart, tailored look of military uniforms. Details, such as padded shoulders, *epaulettes* and piping added variety to an otherwise austere fashion scene. When not in uniform, men wore *double-breasted* jackets, and loose-fitting trousers with *turn-ups*.

Wartime economies

Women's magazines published hints on adapting old clothes and using accessories cleverly, so that one outfit could be worn for daytime and evening. The shortage of stockings inspired some women to put fake tan on their legs and pencil in seams.

The New Look

Two years after the war ended, a designer called **Christian Dior*** launched **The New Look** (also known as the Corolle line). It consisted of a dress with a fitted bodice, flaring at the waist into a full, calf-length skirt. The style created a sensation, because its dramatic lines and extravagant use of fabric contrasted so sharply with the austerity of wartime fashions.

Christian Dior's "New Look".

* You can find out more about **Dior** on page 25.

1950s

The full skirt of **Dior's New Look** continued to be a popular shape in the 50s. Other women's fashions, such as tight-fitting trousers called "pedal pushers" and figure-hugging dresses and suits which tapered towards the knee, emphasized the female shape.

Figure-hugging styles for women.

The lounge suit was a popular item of men's formal wear. Leisure clothes included casual sports jackets and gaudy Hawaiian shirts.

Lounge suit and Hawaiian shirt

Teenage fashion

The prosperity of the 50s meant that people in their teens had a lot of money to spend on clothes. The fashion industry saw an opportunity to create a new market.

Instead of conforming to the same style of dress as their parents, young people wore clothes which reflected their own hobbies and lifestyle. The craze for rock 'n' roll music which started in the USA inspired a new teenage uniform, which rapidly spread abroad.

Boys wore blue jeans, t-shirts and leather jackets or, if they were **Teddy boys**, *drape jackets* based on the Edwardian *frock coat* (see page 6). Girls wore circular skirts, petticoats and tight sweaters, with short white ankle socks and flat pumps.

1960s

Fashion in the 60s was extreme, and the shock value of new designs came to be more important than the cut or quality of the fabric. *Haute couture*, which had dominated the fashion industry until now, was soon eclipsed by *mass market* fashion*.

The early 60s

Men wore smart Italian suits with tapering trousers (drainpipes). This style was popularized by **The Beatles**.

Beatles-style suit

The full figure which had dominated women's fashion in the 50s gave way to a fashion for skinny, boyish looks, reminiscent of the 20s. A British designer called **Mary Quant** popularized mini-skirts, coloured tights and tight sweaters known as "skinny ribs". She also developed a range of "wet-look" garments made from PVC.

Other 60s innovations included see-through blouses and dresses which had shapes cut out of the midriff and futuristic dresses made from plastic chain mail.

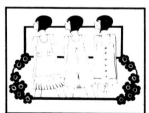
Mary Quant dresses.

The late 60s

Towards the end of the 60s, **unisex** clothes became fashionable. This meant that many clothes could be worn by both sexes. Velvet jackets, bell-bottom trousers, flowery shirts, fringed suede waistcoats and flowing scarves were all popular items.

* You can find out more about *mass market* fashion on page 4.

1970s

The unisex fashions of the late 60s continued into the early 70s. Some people took the haphazard and colourful aspects of unisex dressing and exaggerated them so that they were deliberately tasteless. This style was called **glam rock**, and was adopted by several rock bands. They wore clashing colours, glittery fabrics, lots of make-up, and shoes with enormous platform soles (see below).

Glam rock style

Another trend which became popular with women was a very feminine, countrified style of dress which consisted of long flounced skirts and high-necked blouses in traditional floral prints, worn with crocheted shawls.

In contrast to this look, 1976 brought the rebellion of **punk**. It started in England, inspired by punk-rock bands, and soon spread abroad. Punk was a threatening, unisex look worn mostly by teenagers and its aim was to shock. Punks painted angry slogans on t-shirts and leather jackets and ripped holes in them deliberately. They wore safety pins through their ears and noses, dyed their hair bright unnatural colours, wore pale face make-up and ringed their eyes with black.

Punk style

1980s

80s style has been influenced by several different countries, namely Japan, Britain and the USA.

In the early 80s, **Vivienne Westwood***, an English designer, created the **New Romantic** look. It consisted of pirate-style ruffled shirts, baggy boots and broad leather belts.

Also in the early 80s, Japanese designers such as **Yohji Yamamoto*** and **Rei Kawakubo*** introduced skilfully-cut clothes, whose loose fit and sombre colours were quite austere, yet very stylish.

Dress by Rei Kawakubo from 1984

In the USA, a craze for healthy living and sport inspired designer **Norma Kamali*** to design a range of clothes in sweatshirt fabric (which had previously only been used for sportswear). Her tops with padded shoulders and narrow baggy trousers created a triangular shape, giving the impression of a lean, muscular body. Kamali also designed the rah-rah skirt (see page 23).

In the late 80s, a renewed interest in *haute couture* led to a fashion for 50s styles such as bolero jackets, tight waists and shorter, full skirts. More tailored, skilfully-cut clothes replaced the throw-away styles of the late 70s and early 80s.

* You can find out more about all these designers on pages 26-29.

Inside a fashion studio

Most fashion designers work as part of a team in a studio (workroom). The way a studio works depends on the number of staff employed, the market* it caters for, and whether it specializes in one area of fashion such as knitwear or men's wear.

On these two pages you can find out how a design team develops a range of clothes for one season in the fashion year (this is known as a *collection*). On page 12, you can see how one dress in the collection is designed from start to finish.

The studio

On the right is the fashion studio of a leading British design team called **English Eccentrics**. They produce *designer label** fashion and knitwear in highly original fabrics for both men and women.

Here you can see the fashion designer marking out a *pattern*. Behind her are other members of the studio team. You can find out more about what their jobs involve over the page.

The design team

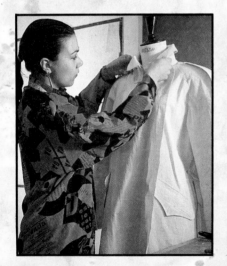

Claire is the company's **fashion designer**. Her job is to design the shape and style of every garment. On pages 12-13 you can see all the stages involved in designing one of them.

Judy is the studio's **knitwear designer**. She sketches shapes for her garments, then works out colour combinations and patterns on a grid. Samples are produced by machine.

Helen is the **fabric designer**. She designs fabrics for Claire to use in her fashion designs. Helen sketches designs on paper, trying out various techniques like *collage* and *marbling***.

* You can find out more about the different markets on page 4.
** The background to these two pages was marbled.

Designing a collection

In fashion, there are two main seasons a year, spring/summer and autumn/winter*. Each season requires a different fashion look and a new range of colours and fabric designs suitable for the time of year (for example, lightweight fabrics in summer, heavier fabrics in winter). To get their designs into the shops at the right time, designers have to work about 12 months in advance, so in spring, the studio will be working on the *collection* for the spring/summer of the following year. As soon as one collection is finished, they begin the next one.

Planning a collection

Every collection is very carefully researched and planned so that all the items in it complement each other, and have the particular fashion look which the company is known for. For example, **English Eccentrics** have made their international reputation designing clothes which are young, daring and witty.

Predicting trends

One of the hardest skills a fashion designer has to master is predicting future trends. To do this, they look at what the fashion directions have been in previous seasons, keep an eye on what others in the fashion business are doing, and read fashion forecasting magazines (see page 56). They also rely on knowledge of their own customers to see which styles succeeded and which were less popular in past seasons. Perhaps most importantly, designers use their imaginations to come up with new ideas. They often choose a theme to provide inspiration.

Choosing a theme

The theme of a collection can be a period in history, a foreign place, a range of colours, a type of fabric—anything which has a strong visual impact.

Vienna 1900

One theme chosen by **English Eccentrics** for a spring/ summer *collection* was **Vienna 1900.** This theme was inspired by an art exhibition held in Paris. Visiting the exhibition gave the designers an insight into the art and culture of the Austrian city at that time and suggested many new ideas for their work.

Here you can see how the rich patterns and vibrant colours of Viennese art (and in particular the work of the artist Gustav Klimt**) inspired **English Eccentrics'** collection. The items around the edges of the book are Helen's original fabric designs and one of Claire's fashion sketches. You can see from these how the golden scrolls and geometric shapes in Klimt's paintings influenced their work. Over the page you can see how one of Helen's fabric designs which resulted from the exhibition research was made into a dress for the spring/summer collection.

---

* You can find out how a fashion designer's year is organized on pages 18-19.
** The book on Gustav Klimt shown above is written by Alessandra Comini and published by Thames & Hudson.

Designing a garment

Having done the groundwork, the design team decides how many and what types of garment should be included in the *collection*. The team has three months to design, produce and publicize the collection in time for their fashion show, where it will be launched before the *fashion buyers* and international press. On these two pages you can see each stage involved in designing a dress for a spring/summer collection, from initial sketch to finished garment.

1. The design

Different designers work in different ways. Some sketch their ideas on paper, others drape fabric on a dress stand, pinning, folding and tucking it until the idea for a garment emerges. Both of these two methods are shown in the photographs on the right. A third method is to adapt their own *patterns* from previous seasons (this method can give continuity to a fashion studio's output). **English Eccentrics**' fashion designer, Claire, usually uses one of the first two methods.

Two-dimensional (2-D) design sketched on paper.

Three-dimensional (3-D) design on a dress stand.

2. Making a paper pattern

Next, Claire makes a rough paper pattern, or life-size 2-D plan, of her garment. To do this, she uses a *block* (a master pattern from which many others can be adapted).

3. Making a toile

A *sample machinist* (or skilled sewing machine operator) then makes a trial version of the dress from plain-coloured cotton jersey. This is called a *toile**.

4. Trying it on

The *toile* is put on to a dress stand (or a model) to see how it fits and whether it hangs properly. Claire makes small adjustments to her original design at this stage.

* *Toiles* are nearly always made from calico, unless the finished garment is in jersey, as here.

5. Making a card pattern

When Claire is completely satisfied with the fit of the *toile*, she shows it to a professional **pattern cutter** who then makes the finished, working version of the pattern out of card. The pattern cutter's job is very precise and painstaking. The fit of the finished garment depends on her accuracy.

6. The finished dress

Finally, a sample dress is made up in the proper fabric. The finished dress will be produced in various different colour combinations (see below).

The fashion show

On the right you can see the finished dress (in one of the alternative **colourways**) as it appeared in the **English Eccentrics** fashion show in the Autumn. The show was part of the **London Designer Collections** for spring/summer of the following year.

The venue for the show and the lighting, props, accessories and make-up were all carefully chosen to accentuate the **Vienna 1900** theme and to make the clothes look as attractive and appealing as possible.

Doing business

English Eccentrics invited international fashion **buyers** and journalists to the show. They consolidated the **catwalk** display by booking a stand in the Olympia exhibition hall (which is the focal point of the London collections). Here, their potential customers could find out all they wanted about garments in the collection, such as colours, delivery dates and prices. The dress in the photograph on the right proved particularly popular. Stocks had sold out by the beginning of spring and a new consignment of dresses had to be produced to meet the demand.

Basic design styles

Most fashion designs are based on certain recurrent shapes and styles. The wider your knowledge of how garments are constructed the more interesting your designs and drawings will be. Here you can see some of the most widely-used styles.

Collars

Peter Pan collar | Mandarin collar | Sailor collar | Shawl collar

Shirt collar | Revers collar | Flat collar | Tie collar

Necklines

Round neck | Square neck | "U" neck | Sweetheart neck | Crossover neck | Boat neck

"V" neck | Scalloped neck | Off-the-shoulder neck | Cowl neck | Scoop neck | Polo neck

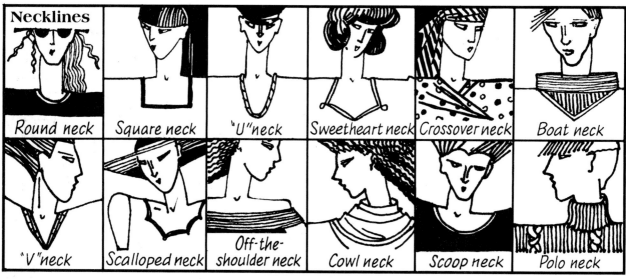

Sleeves

Kimono sleeve | Shirt sleeve | Raglan sleeve

Batwing sleeve | Puff sleeve | Dolman sleeve

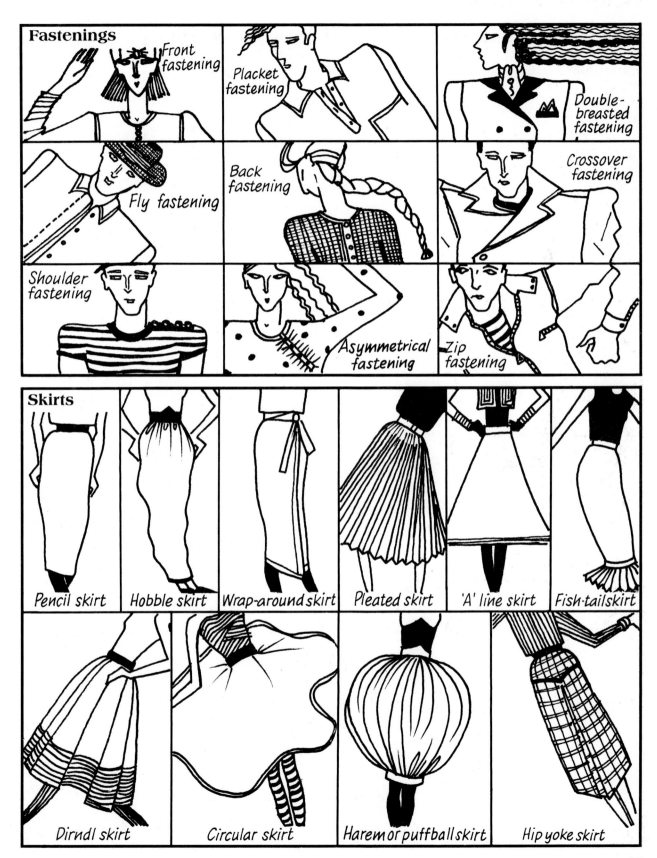

Fastenings

Front fastening

Placket fastening

Double-breasted fastening

Fly fastening

Back fastening

Crossover fastening

Shoulder fastening

Asymmetrical fastening

Zip fastening

Skirts

Pencil skirt

Hobble skirt

Wrap-around skirt

Pleated skirt

'A' line skirt

Fish-tail skirt

Dirndl skirt

Circular skirt

Harem or puffball skirt

Hip yoke skirt

Specializing

Many people in the fashion industry specialize in a particular area, such as men's wear or women's wear. The chart below shows the areas you can specialize in. Opposite, you can see why it is often a good idea to specialize.

Speciality	Sub-sections	Brief	Market	Comments
Women's wear 	Day wear	Practical, comfortable, fashionable.	*Haute couture; designer label; mass market*	Women's fashions change quicker than men's and children's. Styles and colours alter considerably from season to season, especially in the mass market. *Couture* styles tend to be classic and therefore more long-lasting.
	Evening wear	Glamorous, right for the occasion.	*Haute couture;* designer label; mass market	
	Sports wear	Comfortable, well-ventilated, washable.	Mass market; some designer label	
	Lingerie (underwear)	Pretty, washable, comfortable.	Mass market; some designer label	
	Knitwear	Right weight and colour for the season.	Designer label; mass market	
Men's wear 	Day wear	Casual, practical and comfortable.	*Tailoring**; designer label; mass market	Men's fashions tend to change more gradually than women's. On the whole, men's styles and fashion colours are more conservative. Extreme styles can therefore be risky, unless you know your market very well.
	Evening wear	Smart, formal, suitable for the occasion.	Tailoring*; designer label; mass market	
	Sports wear	Comfortable, well-ventilated, washable.	Mass market; some designer label	
	Knitwear	Right weight and colours for the season.	Designer label; mass market	
Children's wear 	Boys' wear	Practical, hardwearing and washable. Not too expensive (as it is quickly outgrown).		Children's clothes should be designed to appeal both to parents (who usually buy the clothes and want them to be practical) and to children who like their clothes to be colourful and fashion-conscious.
	Girls' wear			
	Teenage clothes	Highly fashion-conscious; not too expensive.	Mainly mass market; some designer label	
	Knitwear	Bright, comfortable, washable.		

* This is the traditional men's equivalent of *haute couture*.

Specializing at college

Men's wear by Belinda Coleman

Women's evening wear by Kumars

Women's day wear by Nicollette Marshallsay

Above you can see garments from three *collections* by former students of the **London College of Fashion***. Most students produce a collection in their final year which is then shown to *buyers* and prospective employers at the college show.

To keep costs down, each collection consists of three to eight outfits (the number varies from college to college). To put across a consistent and memorable look within this limited range of garments, students specialize in one area.

Specializing in business

Many professional designers start off by specializing in a particular area of fashion. The smaller and more specific its market, the more likely a company is to get the right look and

feel to their clothes. It is also easier to establish a reputation in the fashion business if people know you for one type of product, rather than several.

When to expand

Once a fashion studio becomes established (that is, has regular orders from *buyers* and is known by the trade and the public), the design team may decide to expand into a new area. If the company has made a name for the clothes it already produces, this helps to sell the new line.

How to expand

It is safest for a company to expand into an area similar to the one it already knows. For example, a designer of men's sports wear might expand into women's sports wear. The design team can ask the advice of their regular buyers about the viability of their proposed new line.

Finding the money

If a company cannot afford to finance its growth it may grant a *licence* to a large clothing manufacturer to use the designer's label in return for payment of an agreed sum of money.

The licensee then pays the design company each time the licence is renewed.

*You can find out more about the **London College of Fashion** on page 62

The fashion year

The fashion year falls into two main seasons, spring/summer and autumn/winter*. Below you can find out how designers plan their time to cope with the seasons' demands. The calendar opposite shows the major fashion events.

Spring/Summer

MAR 1992 — Designer begins *collection*.

OCT 1992 — Collection shown to *buyers*.

FEB 1993 — Collection in shops.

Autumn/Winter

OCT 1992 — Designer begins collection.

MAR 1993 — Collection shown to buyers.

AUG 1993 — Collection in shops.

A typical season

Below you can see a fashion designer's diary for one season.

Fabric exhibition in Frankfurt – designer will attend to choose fabrics for next year's *collection*.

The theme** is the inspiration behind a collection.

Advertising the show in a trade fashion magazine attracts fashion *buyers*.

Invitations are sent to fashion buyers and the press.

Hall in which the fashion show will be held.

OCTOBER
Interstoff – book flight

NOVEMBER
Choose theme Start collection

DECEMBER
Book venue

JANUARY
Book stylist, hairdresser and make-up artist

FEBRUARY
Book ad. in Fashion Focus. Book models. Send out invitations.

MARCH
Show!

18   * Some designers also produce mid-season collections.
    ** You can find out more about themes on page 11.

Below you can see the main events in a typical fashion year, from the legendary *couture* *collections* to international fabric exhibitions and specialist fashion shows.

January

Italian and French *couture* collections for spring/summer (Paris and Rome)

Uomo Italia men's wear and accessories exhibition (Florence)

February

British, Italian and French *ready-to-wear* collections (London, Bologna, Paris)

IMBEX (International men's and boys' wear exhibition) (London)

International men's fashion week (Cologne)

March

British, Italian, American and French designer collections for autumn/winter (London, Milan, New York, Paris)

Munich fashion fair (Munich)

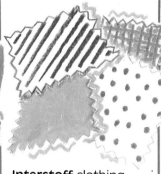

April

Interstoff clothing textiles trade fair (Frankfurt)

May

International designer collections (Tokyo)

London *mid-season* fashion exhibition for autumn

June

Italian children's wear collections (Florence)

Portex: Portuguese ready-to-wear fashion fair for spring/summer (Porto)

July

French and Italian *couture* collections for autumn/winter (Paris, Rome)

Uomo Italia men's wear (Florence)

August

Future Fashions Scandinavia Fair (Copenhagen)

International men's fashion week and international jeans fair (Cologne)

Finnish fashion fair (Helsinki)

September

British, French and American ready-to-wear collections for spring/summer (London, Paris, New York)

Mode enfantine: children's wear exhibition (Paris)

Harrogate fashion fair (England)

October

British, French, American and Italian designer collections for spring/summer (London, Paris, New York, Milan)

Interstoff international textiles and trade fair (Frankfurt)

IGEDO international fashion fair (Dusseldorf)

November

International designer collections (Tokyo)

December

Portex Portuguese ready-to-wear fashion fair for autumn/winter (Porto)

Fashion capitals

Many major cities have lively fashion industries, but only five countries have established truly international reputations in fashion design. These countries are France, Britain, the USA, Italy and Japan. In France, Britain and Japan, the fashion centres are in the capital cities. In the USA and Italy they are in New York and Milan respectively. On these two pages you can find out what makes fashion in each of these countries so special.

Milan

Italian fashions have a reputation for casual elegance and luxurious fabrics. Many Italian *couturiers*, such as **Valentino***, are based in Rome. However, Milan is seen as the fashion capital of Italy because many well-known designers are based there and it is the venue for the Italian *designer collections*, which take place at a big exhibition centre called the **Fiera di Milano** (the Milan Fair). Among the best-known and most exclusive names in

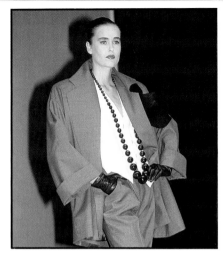

Italian style: casual, stylish daywear in sumptuous fabrics.

Italian fashion design are **Gianfranco Ferre*** (known for his boldly-cut, brightly-coloured clothes), **Giorgio Armani*** (whose subtle, mannish styles for both men and women are his hallmark) and **Gianni Versace*** (famous for his beautifully-cut leatherwear).

Paris

French fashion is chic and stylish. Paris is the home of famous *couture houses*, such as **Dior*** and **Chanel***, who stage exclusive fashion shows in their own *salons*. Many other famous French designers show their work at the *designer collections* which are held twice a year and command international attention. One of the best-known

French designers, and a pioneer of *ready-to-wear* is **Yves Saint Laurent***. He has consistently turned out stylish, quality garments over many years. **Thierry Mugler*** is well-known for his figure-hugging styles and **Karl Lagerfeld**, although a German designer, has a French approach. One of the innovators of French fashion is **Jean-Paul Gaultier***, who designs unusual, witty clothes which stand apart from the main thrust of French style.

Parisian style: sophistication, skilful cutting and smart accessories.

* You can find out more about all these designers on pages 24-29.

London

The British fashion scene is known for unorthodox clothes, with a young market and popular appeal. Recently, London has attracted a lot of international attention with its *designer collections* which are held at a hall called **Olympia**.

Vivienne Westwood* is one of the pioneers of **street style** (the daring, youthful look which London is known for). Following in her wake and turning out fresh ideas consistently, are designers such as **John Galliano, Richmond Cornejo** and **English Eccentrics**. Other well-known names include **Zandra Rhodes*** (fairytale clothes in original fabrics), **Katharine Hamnett*** (slogan t-shirts and chic casuals) and **Bruce Oldfield*** (glamorous evening wear).

British style: young, fresh and innovative.

New York

American fashion design is dominated by a clean-cut, casual style, reflecting the sporty, health-conscious life-styles of many American city dwellers. The fashion industry in New York is based around Seventh Avenue.

A designer who helped to set the trend in America for sport-influenced day wear throughout the 1940s and 50s was **Claire McCardell**. Many of her styles have been revived in the 1980s. More recent influences on the American look have been **Calvin Klein*** (classic coats and separates), **Ralph Lauren*** (casually elegant clothes in natural fabrics), and **Donna Karan*** (practical, sophisticated women's wear).

The American look: casual, sporty lines.

Tokyo

The Japanese "look" is loose and apparently unstructured (though this can often be the result of complicated cutting techniques). Colours are often sombre and subtle and the fabrics used are richly textured.

Many of the famous names in Japanese fashion now work in Europe or the USA, but the Tokyo *designer collections* are still a major international fashion event. Famous names in Japanese fashion include **Kenzo*** (known for layered looks and highly original knitwear); **Issey Miyake*** (a master of draping and cutting) and **Rei Kawakubo*** who developed a completely new way of cutting (this can be compared with the innovation of **Vionnet**** in the 1930s).

Japanese style: loose, unstructured shapes.

* You can find out more about all these designers on pages 24-29.
** You can find out more about **Vionnet** on page 7.

From the catwalk to the high street

On these two pages you can find out how designs find their way from the *catwalks* of the top fashion shows to the racks in the high street shops, and the subtle changes which they undergo *en route*.

Setting the trends

The innovators in fashion traditionally design for the top end of the market, as it is mainly wealthy people who can afford to follow all the latest fashions, without regard to practicality or cost. This means that the top designers can use expensive fabrics and sophisticated production techniques, such as hand-finishing and fancy decoration.

Adapting the trends

*Mass market** designers adapt the trends set by the famous names. They usually wait a season or two to make sure a style is going to catch on before producing their own versions of the original look. To save money and time, they use cheaper fabrics and simpler production techniques which can be done by machine. The end product can therefore be sold more cheaply.

Trend-watching

New *collections* are kept secret until they are offically launched at a fashion show. This prevents other designers from copying and passing designs off as their own. Once a collection is shown, it is virtually impossible to stop it from being copied. Fashion shows are full of reporters taking sketches and photographs, so a fashion "spy" with a sketchbook is inconspicuous. Designers whose work is copied have to accept the practice as a fact of life, as it is so difficult to prove that their copyright has been infringed (see opposite).

* You can find out more about the mass market on page 4.

Spot the difference

Here you can see how a mass market designer might adapt a "designer original" to cut costs and production time and to give the garment a wider appeal.

Designer original

Fully lined, double-breasted, three-quarter length jacket in wool/cashmere.

Mass market version

Jacket is same basic shape, but made from wool/synthetic fabric and unlined.

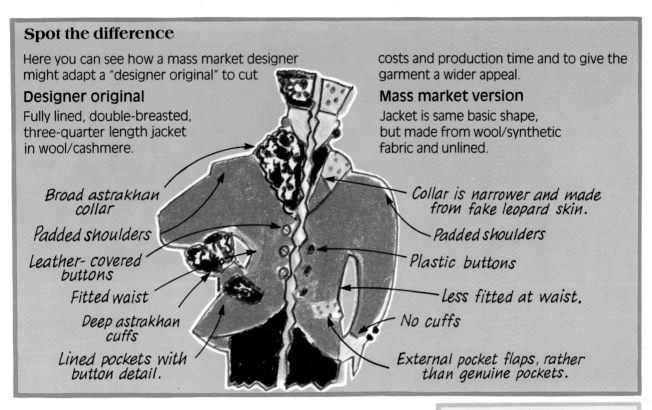

Broad astrakhan collar

Padded shoulders

Leather-covered buttons

Fitted waist

Deep astrakhan cuffs

Lined pockets with button detail.

Collar is narrower and made from fake leopard skin.

Padded shoulders

Plastic buttons

Less fitted at waist.

No cuffs

External pocket flaps, rather than genuine pockets.

Famous copies

Below are two examples of designer styles which have been copied for the *mass market*.

When Lady Diana Spencer married the Prince of Wales in 1981, her **Emanuel** dress was copied by mass market designers, who worked through the night to get cheaper replicas into the shops by the next day.

Norma Kamali's rah rah skirt was one of the most widely imitated designs of the 1980s. It was easy for high street manufacturers to copy because it was a simple design made in inexpensive sweatshirting fabric.

Copyright

In 1861 a French craft guild known as the **Chambre Syndicale de la Haute Couture** was set up to protect *couturiers* against infringement of copyright (other designers stealing their ideas). Today, even though designs can be officially registered, breaches of copyright are difficult to prove for two reasons. Firstly, the same shapes recur continually in fashion, often appearing in the work of several different designers at once, making it difficult to establish who originated them. Secondly, a designer only has to change a detail, to claim that his/her design is a different one and that no copyright laws have been infringed.

A-Z of fashion design

On the next six pages you can find out about the careers and personal hallmarks of some of the world's top fashion designers, from the late greats, such as **Chanel** and **Dior**, to rising stars like **Jean-Paul Gaultier**.

A

Alaia, Azzedine

Dates: unknown
Nationality: Tunisian

Career: studied in Tunis. Worked for **Dior**, **Laroche** and **Mugler**, then set up on his own.

Hallmarks: clingy, seductive women's wear in leather and viscose.

Outfit by **Georgio Armani**

Armani, Georgio

Dates: 1935-
Nationality: Italian

Career: designed for **Cerruti** and **Ungaro**, before launching his own label. Began with men's wear, moved into women's wear.

Hallmarks: elegant, uncluttered day wear for men and women.

B

Balenciaga, Cristobal

Dates: 1895-1972
Nationality: Spanish

Career: trained as a tailor. Opened his own salon in San Sebastian, then moved to Paris. Particularly influential in the 40s and 50s.

Hallmarks: superbly cut women's wear.

Design by **Pierre Balmain**

Balmain, Pierre

Dates: 1914-1982
Nationality: French

Career: no formal training. Worked for **Molyneux** and **Lelong**, before opening his own *house* in 1945.

Hallmarks: versatility. Designed elegant day, evening and sports wear.

Beene, Geoffrey

Dates: 1927-
Nationality: American

Career: studied in New York. Worked in Paris, then returned to USA to work in *ready-to-wear*. Set up his own company in 1963.

Hallmarks: witty fantasy garments, in opulent fabrics.

C

Cardin, Pierre

Dates: 1922-
Nationality: French

Career: started as tailor's assistant. Designed theatrical costumes and men's wear, then expanded into women's wear.

Hallmarks: dramatic *collections* with unifying themes.

Chanel, Coco *

Dates: 1883-1971
Nationality: French

Career: worked in a hat shop. Opened two dress shops, and later her own *fashion house* in Paris.

Hallmarks: classic women's wear in colours such as navy and beige.

House of Chanel

Courrèges, André

Dates: 1923-
Nationality: French

Career: left career as civil engineer to become a designer. Worked for **Balenciaga**; started own *house* in 1961.

Hallmarks: stark, space-age designs of the 60s.

* Her real name was **Gabrielle Chanel**.

D de la Renta, Oscar

Dates: 1932-
Nationality: Dominican

Career: originally a painter. Worked for **Balenciaga**. Went to Paris, then New York, where he set up his own business.

Hallmarks: exotic and elaborate evening gowns.

House of Dior

Dior, Christian

Dates: 1905-1957
Nationality: French

Career: no formal training. Worked with designers **Piguet** and **Lelong**, until he got financial backing for his own company. Presented his first collection in 1947.

Hallmarks: classic *haute couture.*

E Ellis, Perry

Dates: 1940-1987
Nationality: American

Career: studied retailing and business. Worked in sportswear from 1968; own label 1978. Own company from 1980, when he went into day wear.

Hallmarks: classics in natural fabrics.

F Fendi (company)

Dates: Founded 1918
Nationality: Italian

History: founded by **Adele Fendi** and run since by her five daughters Paola, Alda, Franca, Carla and Anna and their families.

Hallmarks: opulent fur clothing.

Ferre, Gianfranco

Dates: 1944-
Nationality: Italian

Career: qualified as an architect, but became designer of jewellery and accessories, then day wear and sports wear. Own house from 1978.

Hallmarks: chic, well-cut clothes.

Outfit by Gianfranco Ferre

Fiorucci, Elio

Dates: 1935-
Nationality: Italian

Career: ran family shoe shop from 1962. Expanded into clothes, supervising his own design team in Milan.

Hallmarks: fun clothes and accessories for the young.

G Gaultier, Jean-Paul

Dates: 1952-
Nationality: French

Career: Started sketching designs in his teens. Worked for **Cardin** and **Patou**. Own business from 1977.

Hallmarks: young, often daring, ready-to-wear designs.

Outfit by Bill Gibb

Gibb, Bill

Dates: 1943-1988
Nationality: Scottish

Career: trained at St Martin's School of Art, and the RCA*, London. Designed for **Baccaret**. Own firm during the 70s. Then returned to freelance work.

Hallmarks: lavish evening gowns.

Gigli, Romeo

Dates: 1950-
Nationality: Italian

Career: trained as an architect. Started work as a fashion designer in New York, returning to Milan to form his own company.

Hallmarks: soft, romantic, women's wear.

* Royal College of Art. For more information, see pages 62-63).

H

Halston, Roy

Dates: 1932-
Nationality: American

Career: started in *millinery*. Opened own ready-to-wear business in 1966. Has designed dance costumes.

Hallmarks: knitwear and figure-hugging clothes in jersey.

Hamnett, Katharine

Dates: 1948-
Nationality: English

Career: trained at St Martin's School of Art, London. Worked freelance. Own business from 1979.

Hallmarks: slogan t-shirts and workwear. Revived 1950s styles in late 80s.

J

Jackson, Betty

Dates: 1940-
Nationality: English

Career: Worked as illustrator. Later, designed for **Wendy Dagworthy**, **Quorum** and **Coopers**. Own company from 1981.

Hallmarks: striking, yet practical women's wear.

Women's wear by Betty Jackson

K

Kamali, Norma

Dates: 1945-
Nationality: American

Career: studied in New York. Opened shop selling own designs in 1967. New company, with a more sporty direction from 1978.

Hallmarks: use of jersey fabrics.

Outfit by Norma Kamali

Karan, Donna

Dates: 1948-
Nationality: American

Career: Trained in New York. Worked for **Addenda** and **Anne Klein** (specializing in sports wear). Set up her own company in 1984.

Hallmarks: seductive, clingy clothes such as **the bodysuit**.

Outfit by Donna Karan

Kawakubo, Rei

Dates: 1942-
Nationality: Japanese

Career: worked for textile company in Japan from 1964-1966. Then became a freelance designer. Started **Comme des Garçons** in 1969.

Hallmarks: original, sculptured designs, intricately cut.

Outfit by Rei Kawakubo

Kenzo*

Dates: 1940-
Nationality: Japanese

Career: studied art in Japan, then worked as a pattern designer for a magazine. Moved to Paris and worked freelance. Opened shop selling own designs in 1970.

Hallmarks: innovative knitwear.

Klein, Calvin

Dates: 1942-
Nationality: American

Career: studied in New York. Started by designing *outer wear*. Own business from 1968. Later went into sports and day wear.

Hallmarks: sophisticated clothes in natural fabrics.

*Kenzo's real name is Kenzo Takada.

Lagerfeld, Karl

Dates: 1938-
Nationality: German

Career: Worked in Paris for **Balmain** and **Patou**, then went freelance. Design director for **Chanel** from 1983. Own label from 1984.

Hallmarks: bold, often witty designs.

Lanvin, Jeanne

Dates: 1867-1946
Nationality: French

Career: trained as a dressmaker and *milliner,* and ran her own Paris hat shop. Went into dressmaking, then opened her own *house.*

Hallmarks: mother and daughter outfits.

Outfit by **Lauren**

Lauren, Ralph

Dates: 1939-
Nationality: American

Career: studied business in New York. Designed men's wear, expanded into women's wear, then started own company.

Hallmarks: casual, sophisticated clothes in natural fabrics.

M

Missoni (company)

Dates: founded 1953
Nationality: Italian

History: run by husband and wife, **Tai** and **Rosita Missoni.** They started their own knitwear label after selling freelance at first.

Hallmarks: glamorous knitwear.

Miyake, Issey

Dates: 1935-
Nationality: Japanese

Career: studied fashion in Paris. Worked for **Laroche, Givenchy** and **Geoffrey Beene.** Own label since 1971.

Hallmarks: rich textures, and bold geometric shapes.

Outfit by **Claude Montana**

Montana, Claude

Dates: 1949-
Nationality: French

Career: designed jewellery. Then worked for leather company in Paris. Launched own *collection* in 1977.

Hallmarks: bold, assertive clothes, often in leather.

Mori, Hanae

Dates: 1926-
Nationality: Japanese

Career: studied in Japan. Designed film costumes, and from 1955, fashions for her own shop. Moved to New York in 1977, where she opened her own *fashion house.*

Hallmarks: oriental-style evening wear.

Mugler, Thierry

Dates: 1948-
Nationality: French

Career: worked as a window dresser in Paris. First designed under the **Café de Paris** label. Started his own label in 1973.

Hallmarks: dramatic, figure-hugging women's wear.

Outfit by **Jean Muir** 1975

Muir, Jean

Dates: 1933-
Nationality: Scottisn

Career: sketched clothes for **Liberty***. Moved to **Jaeger** and designed own range of clothes for them. Own company from 1966.

Hallmarks: soft, classic clothes in jersey and suede.

---

* A London department store

Oldfield, Bruce

Dates: 1950-
Nationality: English

Career: trained at Ravensbourne College of Art* and St Martin's School of Art*. Then worked as a freelance designer. First *collection* 1975.

Hallmarks: chic evening wear.

Dress from the Bruce Oldfield collection

Patou, Jean

Dates: 1880-1936
Nationality: French

Career: worked in his uncle's fur business. In 1912, he opened a dressmaker's. Closed this during the First World War, but reopened it in 1919.

Hallmarks: simple, well-cut classics.

Outfit by **Jean Patou**

Quant, Mary

Dates: 1934-
Nationality: English

Career: worked for a *milliner*, then opened **Bazaar**, a shop which sold her own lines.

Hallmarks: bright, original, inexpensive clothes aimed at the young.

1960s dresses by **Mary Quant**

Rhodes, Zandra

Dates: 1940-
Nationality: English

Career: studied at Royal College of Art*, London. Printed own textiles, which she made into dresses and sold. Own *house* from 1968.

Hallmarks: exotic fantasy dresses.

Dress from the **Zandra Rhodes** collection

Saint Laurent, Yves

Dates: 1936-
Nationality: French

Career: studied in Paris. Worked as head designer for **Dior**. Own *house* from 1962. Pioneered *ready-to-wear*.

Hallmarks: casually stylish city clothes.

Outfit by **Saint Laurent**

Schiaparelli, Elsa

Dates: 1890-1973
Nationality: Italian

Career: studied philosophy. Designed and sold knitwear before first opening a shop, and then later her own *fashion house.*

Hallmarks: witty, imaginative designs.

Tarlazzi, Angelo

Dates: 1945-
Nationality: Italian

Career: worked for **Carosa** in Italy, then for **Patou** in Paris, eventually becoming the company's artistic director. Own *house* from 1978.

Hallmarks: soft, fluid, women's wear.

U

Ungaro, Emanuel

Dates: 1933-
Nationality: Italian

Career: learned tailoring with the family business. Worked for **Balenciaga** and **Courrèges**. Own business from 1965.

Hallmarks: bold, sumptuous fabrics.

V

Valentino*

Dates: 1933-
Nationality: Italian

Career: studied in Milan and Paris. Worked in Paris with **Desses** and **Laroche**, before returning to Italy in 1959 to start his own *fashion house*.

Hallmarks: glamorous *couture* garments.

Outfit by Gianni Versace

Versace, Gianni

Dates: 1946-
Nationality: Italian

Career: worked with his mother (who was a dressmaker), then for **Genny** and **Complice**. Own *fashion house* from 1978.

Hallmarks: elegant, well-cut clothes, often made from leather.

W

Westwood, Vivienne

Dates: 1941-
Nationality: English

Career: trained as teacher. Opened shop, "World's End", selling punk clothes in 70s. Several influential *collections* since.

Hallmarks: shocking theme collections.

Two designs from the **House of Worth**

Worth, House of

Dates: 1858-1954
Nationality: French

History: started by **Charles Frederick Worth**, the first *couturier*, and run by his sons when he died. Taken over by the **House of Paquin** in 1954.

Hallmarks: gowns for society ladies.

Y

Yamamoto, Yohji

Dates: 1943-
Nationality: Japanese

Career: studied fashion in Tokyo. Worked freelance, then started his own company in 1972.

Hallmarks: innovative, loosely cut clothes.

Outfit by Yamamoto

Yuki**

Dates: 1937-
Nationality: Japanese

Career: trained as textile designer, architect and fashion designer. Worked for **Feraud**, **Michael**, **Hartnell** and **Cardin**. Own business from 1973.

Hallmarks: flowing jersey dresses.

Z

Zoran, Ladicorbic

Dates: 1947-
Nationality: Yugoslavian

Career: qualified as architect. Moved to New York. Own *collections* since 1977.

Hallmarks: stark designs in luxurious fabrics.

* Real name, **Valentino Garavani**.
** Real name, **Gnyuki Torimaru**.

What is fashion illustration?

Fashion illustration (or fashion drawing) is a way of presenting clothes on figures, so that they look as attractive and glamorous as possible. Newspapers and magazines use fashion drawings to show the latest styles. Advertisers use them to sell clothes.

How do illustrations differ from designs?

This is a fashion design. It is a simple, diagrammatic sketch showing in detail, with notes, how the garment should be constructed.

This is a fashion illustration of the same garment. It shows the basic style, without the same amount of detail. It also projects a good fashion image.

The beginnings of fashion illustration

The first fashion illustrations were called fashion plates. They were published in magazines from about 1770 onwards. At this time, only wealthy women could afford to have fashionable clothes made for them. In 1840 the sewing machine was invented and this meant that clothes could be mass-produced. The interest in fashion magazines became more widespread, and the need for fashion illustration was established. These days, many magazines use photographs instead of illustrations. However, the best of them use a mixture, so there is still work around for fashion illustrators.

Working as a fashion illustrator

To be a fashion illustrator you need to be good at drawing figures. You should love fashion, have a strong colour sense and the ability to draw clothes stylishly and with attention to detail. You must also be able to work to a *brief* and meet *deadlines* (deliver work on time). You can find out more about working as a fashion illustrator on pages 56-57.

Fashion illustration as a hobby

You may like to draw and even design your own clothes as a hobby. This gives you the freedom to draw the clothes you like (you could even design your ideal wardrobe). It can also be good practice if you think you may want to become a fashion illustrator. You can discover many of the basic techniques of fashion illustration on pages 36-41.

Famous fashion illustrators

Some of the greatest fashion illustrators were at work in the 1920s and 30s, before photography became the dominant medium in fashion. Look out for names such as **Erté, Georges Barbier, Helen Dryden** and **André Marty.** You can see their work in books on fashion illustration (see page 62) and in old magazines, such as **La Gazette du Bon Ton*, Vogue** and **Harper's Bazaar.**

Later artists to look out for include **Carl Erickson, René Bouché** and **Antonio.**

Drawing by **Erté** for **Harper's Bazaar**

Drawing by **Barbier** for **La Gazette du Bon Ton**

* La Gazette du Bon Ton was a French fashion magazine founded in 1912.

Inspiration

Many different factors contribute to the style and mood of a fashion illustration. Obviously, the clothes you choose to draw will dominate your illustration, but other things such as the pose of the figure, the colours and textures you use, and whether you have a plain or decorative background, will also affect the "mood" of your drawing. On this page are some hints on gathering inspiration for the different aspects of your drawing.

Fashion and clothes

Look in shops and costume museums and notice the changing shape of clothes. Try to find out about fashion in the past as well as now.

Art and crafts

Paintings, sculptures and pottery can provide ideas for fabric design and decoration in your drawings. Sketch any patterns which appeal to you.

Film and video

Notice the backgrounds, colours and lighting effects used in films and videos. This can help you create a "mood" for your drawing.

Books and magazines

Fashion magazines (especially Italian or French ones), and books on costume and fashion will give you ideas for shapes and styles of clothes.

Fabric

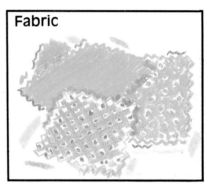

Notice the textures, colours and patterns of fabric and think about the type of clothes they would be suitable for. Save scraps of fabric which appeal to you.

Making a scrap book

You could keep a scrap book of all the bits and pieces you want to save, such as clippings from magazines, bits of fabric, sketches etc.

Buy about ten sheets of strong A2 paper (it can be white or coloured). Put all the sheets together and fold them in half widthwise.

Punch* holes close to the folded edge, as shown and thread cord or ribbon through them. Now stick pictures and fabrics inside.

* If you are using thick paper, you may need to punch the holes in two batches.

Materials

On these two pages you can find out about the various materials you can use for fashion illustration. Most of them are easy to use and inexpensive. You can see examples of the effects you can achieve with these materials on pages 42-53.

Watercolour paint comes in tubes or small blocks, called pans. You mix it with water before using it. It has a fluid, translucent look which is good for loose, flowing styles of illustration (see page 42).

Gouache paint comes in tubes and jars*. It can be used as it is, or mixed with water. Gouache gives a flat, bold effect which is good for *graphic* styles of fashion illustration (such as that on page 47).

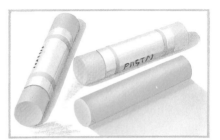

Artist's pastels are chalky sticks of colour. They come in three grades of softness and are quite expensive to buy. They can be worked (smudged and blended) on the paper to produce soft, hazy effects.

Oil pastels are sticks of colour, like artist's pastels, but they make much thicker, bolder marks. Oil pastel can be used as it is, or it can be spread and softened with petrol once it is on the paper (see page 51).

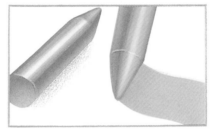

Wax crayons are harder and more translucent than oil pastels. It is worth paying a bit more for good ones, as they cover the paper more thickly. You can see a good way to use them on page 43.

Fibre-tip pens or **markers** come in many sizes, from very fine (good for outlines and detail) to very broad (for large areas of colour). Choose a good variety of colours and thicknesses to start with.

Drawing inks come in a wide range of colours. They can be put on with a brush, and used like watercolour (as on page 45), or with a fountain or dip pen for a tighter, more controlled style of drawing.

Coloured pencils combine well with watercolour or pastel. Thick, grainy ones are best for fashion drawing. Water-soluble pencils can be blended, once on the page, by putting a wash over the top.

Water-soluble crayons are chunky sticks of colour which you can blend, by adding water, to give a paint-like effect. Alternatively, use them on their own like ordinary crayons, for a thick, bold line.

Pencils

Pencils are graded for hardness or softness with letters and numbers. Below are some examples.

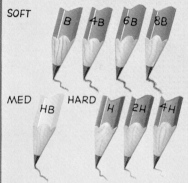

SOFT — B 4B 6B 8B

MED — HB   HARD — H 2H 4H

Soft pencils are best for most types of fashion drawing. They make thick, grainy marks which rub out easily. Hard pencils give a faint, neat line which is good for very tight styles of illustration (such as that on page 47).

Chinagraph pencils have a waxy texture which gives a thick, bold line on paper.

Charcoal and conté

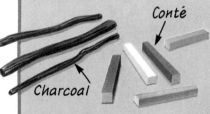

Conté

Charcoal

These are both soft, smudgy media which are good for life drawings and figurative styles of fashion drawing. Charcoal comes in brittle sticks, conté in stick or pencil form. Always use a fixative to stop your finished drawing smudging.

Paper

There are many different types and weights of paper available. You can buy it in pads or single sheets, in various standard sizes (see page 35). Below you can see some of the most useful types of paper for fashion illustration.

Cartridge paper is cheap, smooth, white or cream paper. Use lightweight, unstretched cartridge for pencil, pen and wax crayon. Use heavier, stretched* cartridge paper for watercolour, gouache and ink.

Watercolour paper is quite costly. It comes in three textures, H.P. (smooth), NOT (slightly rougher) and Rough. If using a lightweight paper, stretch* it first. Heavier ones can be used unstretched.

Layout paper is cheap, lightweight paper which is good for rough work such as sketching.

Marker paper is lightweight, with a bleed-proof surface to stop fibre tip pens or markers from running. Do not use marker paper if you are also using a wetter medium, such as ink, as the paper will *cockle.*

Coloured paper is good for making collages. You can buy various kinds. Cover paper comes in a wide range of colours. Tissue paper and pictures cut from old magazines are also useful for collage. There are some more ideas on page 48.

You can buy special **Pastel paper** with a rough surface which takes grainy textures well. It is useful for artist's pastel, conté and charcoal.

Sugar paper is cheap, rough paper which comes in lots of bold colours. You can use it for charcoal, conté, pastel and chalk.

Self-adhesive film

Self-adhesive film, such as **Letratone**, comes in many different patterns and is good for giving an impression of garment texture. You can find out how to use it on page 45. On the right are some examples of textures you can simulate using Letratone.

Mohair

Rubber

Tweed

Jersey

---

* You can see how to stretch paper on page 35.

Equipment

On these two pages you can see the equipment you need for fashion illustration. Most of it is inexpensive, except for the light box (see opposite).

Paint brushes

Brushes come in different sizes, shapes and textures. The best ones are made from animal hair (such as sable) or bristle, but you can also buy cheaper synthetic ones. There are three basic brush shapes. The round ones are the best for fashion illustration. Square brushes can be useful for painting backgrounds.

Shapes

Round   Filbert   Square

Brushes are graded in numbers, from the finest 0000, to the thickest, 20. Not all types of brush cover the whole range. It is best to start off with two fine, one thick and about three medium brushes.

Sizes

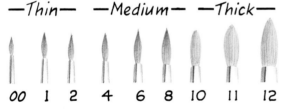

—Thin—   —Medium—   —Thick—

00 1 2 4 6 8 10 11 12

Other painting equipment

Rag for cleaning brushes and so on.

Old newspaper to protect surfaces.

Sponge for textured paint techniques.

Palette or saucer for mixing paint.

Jar of water — to thin paints and rinse brushes.

Masking tape for paint techniques and collage.

General equipment

The items below are useful for various types of illustration, as well as mounting your work.

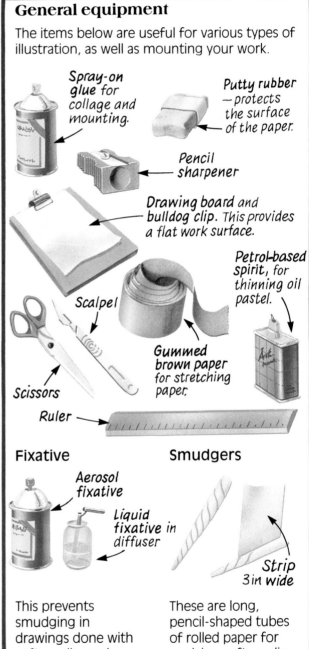

Spray-on glue for collage and mounting.

Putty rubber — protects the surface of the paper.

Pencil sharpener

Drawing board and bulldog clip. This provides a flat work surface.

Petrol-based spirit, for thinning oil pastel.

Scalpel

Gummed brown paper for stretching paper.

Scissors

Ruler

Fixative

Aerosol fixative

Liquid fixative in diffuser

This prevents smudging in drawings done with soft media, such as pastel or conté. It comes in aerosol or liquid form. Liquid is cheaper, but you will need a **diffuser** to apply it.

Smudgers

Strip 3 in wide

These are long, pencil-shaped tubes of rolled paper for applying soft media, such as charcoal or pastel. Buy them from art shops, or make your own, by rolling up a strip of A4 cartridge paper.

Using a light box

A light box is useful for tracing a rough sketch on to thicker paper. The light shines through the thicker paper, showing the sketch beneath. They can be costly, so you may decide to make a cheaper version.

Home-made light box

You will need a cheap plastic or wooden picture frame at least 12" x 16"; a piece of toughened ¼" safety glass* cut to fit the frame (ask the glass merchant to do this for you); some thick books and an angle-poise lamp.

1

Rest either end of the framed glass on an even pile of books, distributing the weight of the glass evenly at each end.

2

Carefully position the angle-poise lamp so that the light bulb is shining up from underneath on to the glass, as shown.

Stretching paper

If you want to use watercolour or inks on lightweight paper**, stretch it first to stop it from *cockling* when the paint dries.

You will need a large piece of hardboard, a roll of gummed brown paper, a sponge, a clean cloth, a ruler, a scalpel, a bowl of water and a sheet of paper.

1

Put your paper in the centre of the hardboard. Wet it evenly all over with the dampened sponge.

2

Smooth the paper flat with the cloth, working from the centre outwards. Stick the edges down with gummed paper.

3

When the paper is completely dry, cut it off the hardboard with a scalpel, using a ruler to keep the edges straight.

Paper sizes

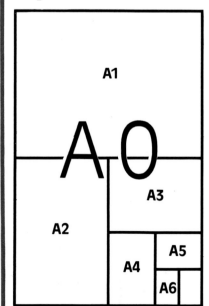

The most commonly used system of sizing paper is based on a sheet of paper with an area of one square metre (known as the A0 size). This is divided into six smaller sizes (see diagram) ranging from A1 which is half the A0 size to A6 which is 1/64th of the A0 size.

Generally, A2 is the best size to use for practising life drawing and for "loose" styles of fashion drawing. For your portfolio, and for commercial work, A3 may be more practical (it is also cheaper to buy or make an A3 size light box – see left).

---

* This type of glass is safe to use as long as the edges are protected by a frame.
** This includes layout paper or lightweight cartridge or watercolour paper.

Figure drawing

Clothes are usually displayed on models because this shows them off to their best advantage. If you want to do fashion illustration, it is therefore vital to learn how to draw well-proportioned figures.

The next four pages show you the techniques, from the basic construction of the figure, to a more detailed finished drawing.

Drawing from life

Your model should hold the pose for about 20 minutes.

A good way to learn figure drawing is to go to a *life drawing* class, where you will be able to draw from a nude model. This teaches you about the structure of the body. Alternatively, ask a friend to pose for you, in close fitting clothes. Then sketch him or her as shown on the next page.

Practising without a model

If you want to practise figure drawing and you cannot find anyone to model for you, here are some alternatives. You should not use them as a substitute for *life drawing*, but they are helpful because you can spend as long as you like getting the proportions and details exactly right. They will also help to improve your technique when you do have the chance to draw from life.

Magazines

You can draw figures from photographs in magazines. Resist the temptation to trace them, as your finished drawing will look flat. Prop the magazine in front of you and imagine that you are looking at a real person. Choose clear, well-lit photos showing full-length figures in interesting poses.

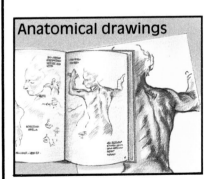

Anatomical drawings

Try copying the anatomical drawings of **Leonardo** and **Michelangelo***. This will help you learn the positions of bones, joints and muscles.

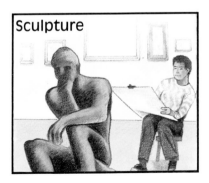

Sculpture

Draw from classical nude sculptures in your local art gallery. You can study them from all angles and spend time getting the details exactly right.

Self-portraits

Look at your face in a mirror and draw it. Or draw your own hands and feet. This will help you when you come to add details to your life drawing.

* Ask in your local library for art books containing this type of drawing.

Doing a figure drawing

When drawing from life, keep glancing at your model. The guidelines below will help you to put down what you see. Do not worry about getting the proportions exactly right. Instead, try to draw quickly and confidently. Your technical skill will improve gradually with practice.

Materials

You will need a soft pencil (6B, 7B, or 8B), an oil or artist's pastel (any colour), some sheets of A2 cartridge paper, a putty rubber, a drawing board and a bulldog clip.

Preparation

Sit far enough away from your model to enable you to see the whole figure easily. Clip the paper to your drawing board and prop it in front of you, at arm's length. Break off about 1 inch of pastel.

Method

1. Look at the angle of your model's head. Use the edge of your pastel to shade it in on your paper. This is called **blocking in.**

2. Look at the angle of the shoulders in relation to the head. Draw a pencil line to represent them. This is known as a **construction mark.**

3. Using your pastel, block in the neck (as you did the head), at right angles to the shoulders.

Right angle

Position of shoulders

CF line

Position of elbow

Right angle

Position of hand

Position of feet

4. Imagine a line running through the centre of your model, parallel to the backbone, from shoulders to waist. It may be curved, as here, depending on the model's pose. This is called the **centre front (CF)** line. Mark it in pencil. Look at the angle of the model's waist. Mark the waistline on your drawing. It should be at right angles to the CF line in the hip area.

5. Block in the upper part of the body from shoulders to waist (rib cage area) in pastel. The edges should be almost parallel to the CF line.

6. Look at your model and see what direction the imaginary CF line takes from the waist to the top of the legs. Extend the CF line on your drawing. Block in the hip area, in the same way as you did the rib cage area.

7. Before you draw the legs, look at the position of your model's feet in relation to his/her head. Make construction marks where they come. Do the same for the knees. Then block in the legs and feet.

8. Look at the position of your model's hands and elbows. Make construction marks where they come, then block in the arms and hands, as for the legs and feet.

Now you have the basic framework of your drawing. You can see how to develop it on the next page.

Adding line

Once you have put the basic shape of your model down on paper, you can use your pencil to outline the torso and limbs and position the features. This is known as *adding line.* You should still keep looking at your model as the main source of information.

Method

1. Look at your model's head. Now outline it over the top of the oblong block in your first sketch.

2. Draw a *centre front (CF)* line from the top of the head to the chin.

3. Next you find the position for the eyes. If you are looking at your model straight on, draw a *construction mark* half-way down the CF line. If you are looking at your model from above or below, the construction mark for the eyes will be further down or up, as in **b** or **c** above. Then extend the mark into a line running right across the face.

4. Notice the position of your model's nose and mouth. Make two construction marks on your CF line where they come. Now extend the marks into lines running right across the face.

5. Mark the position of the ears either side of the head, between the construction lines for the eyes and nose.

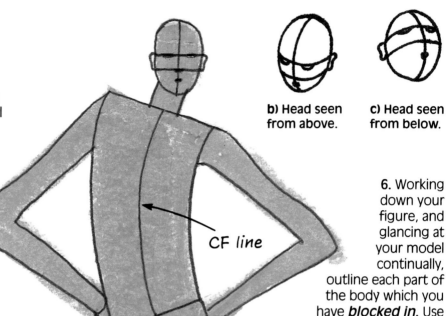

b) Head seen from above.

c) Head seen from below.

CF line

6. Working down your figure, and glancing at your model continually, outline each part of the body which you have *blocked in.* Use the blocked-in figure as a guide, improving on its shape and correcting any mistakes which you have made.

Back view Using the backbone as your guide, draw in a *centre back* line . Then use the same method as before to draw the figure.

Side view Mark in an imaginary line parallel to the model's backbone, going through the centre of the body from shoulders to waist. Then continue as before.

Proportion

Now that you know the basic technique of figure drawing, you can practise getting the proportions right. Below are some rough guidelines for drawing men, women and children. You do not have to use the "head count" shown below. Some fashion illustrators use a higher one.

Man

Eight heads high – head is bigger than a woman's, therefore figure is taller.

Woman

Eight heads high. Head is smaller than a man's. Therefore figure is shorter.

Child

The child's figure varies from four to six heads high according to age. At first the head is quite big in relation to the body, but as a child gets older the "head count" increases.

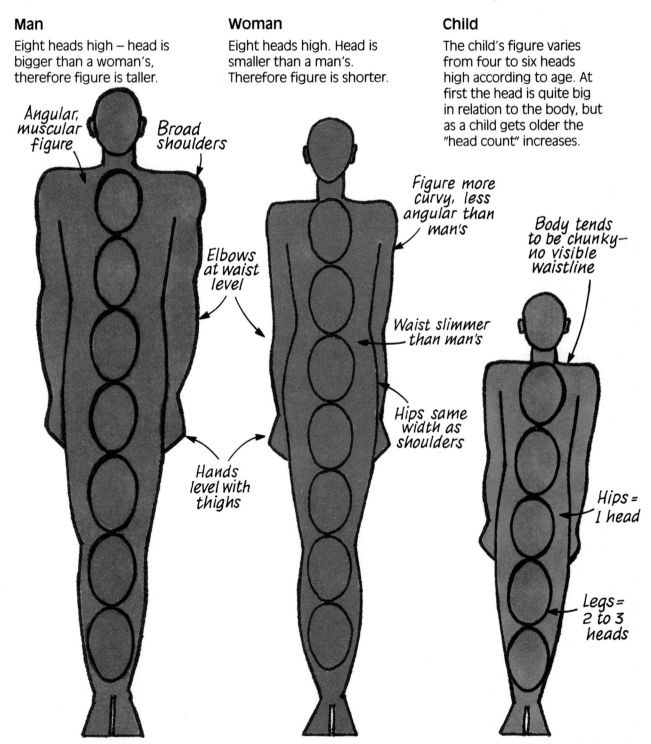

Angular, muscular figure

Broad shoulders

Elbows at waist level

Hands level with thighs

Figure more curvy, less angular than man's

Waist slimmer than man's

Hips same width as shoulders

Body tends to be chunky – no visible waistline

Hips = 1 head

Legs = 2 to 3 heads

Fashion illustration

When you have practised several figure drawings, the next stage in learning fashion illustration is to sketch a clothed figure. You may now know enough about basic anatomy and proportion to **block in** the rough shape without **construction marks**. You can then **add line**, developing your style with an eye for detail and texture as you progress.

Composition

Your figure's pose and position on the page are known as **composition**. A good way to compose* your drawing is to look at your model through a matchbox cover. Ask him/her to adopt poses suitable to the style of dress. Imagine the sides of the matchbox cover are the edges of your paper, and choose a pose which makes good use of the space. Below are some suggestions.

Women's day wear: casual standing or sitting poses.

Sports wear: active poses which convey health and vigour.

Evening wear: elegant, sophisticated lounging poses.

Men's day wear: debonair standing or sitting poses.

Drawing your figure

When you have decided on a pose for your model and the position of your drawing on the page, you can begin getting the basic shape down on paper, following the instructions below.

Materials

You will need the same materials as you used for figure drawing: a soft pencil (6B, 7B or 8B), some A2 cartridge paper, a putty rubber, drawing board and a bulldog clip. However, instead of one pastel for blocking in, you need a selection of coloured pastels (including a flesh colour** for the skin).

Blocking in

Firstly, use your flesh-coloured pastel to block in the parts of the model where flesh is visible (such as the head, hands and legs). If the limbs are covered by garments, such as tights or a long-sleeved dress, use a coloured pastel to block them in. Then block in the garments in the appropriate colours.

* If drawing from a photograph, your choice of poses will be more limited.

** Use a dark flesh-tone if drawing summer clothes or swimwear.

Adding line

When you have blocked in the shape of your figure you can define it with line, as follows:

Face and features

With your pencil, draw in the features, starting with the nose. Draw faint construction lines first if you do not feel confident positioning the features without them (see page 38). Then outline the shape of the face. Do not make your drawing too fussy (this is known as *overworking*). Use pastel or coloured pencil to add colour as you go along; that way you will be able to concentrate better and your drawing will flow.

Hair

Draw a block of solid pastel for the hair. You can add a bit of line for interest, but do not overwork it, as this will distract attention from the rest of your drawing.

Clothes

Now add line to the garments, refining the shapes you blocked in. Remember that most professional fashion drawings are done to sell clothes, so make sure you draw them accurately and attractively. Notice the "cut" of the clothes (their shape, length and fullness) and try to reproduce them as well as you can in your drawing.

Solid pastel–
minimum
of detail

Pattern
of fabric
distorted
by body
shape.

Add detail
in pencil or
coloured
pencil.

Fabric

When drawing patterned fabric, such as the stripes on the top and skirt shown here, remember that the pattern will be distorted by the model's shape. Your drawing will look more three-dimensional if you draw the pattern as you see it, rather than drawing it as if it were flat.

Detail

Next, look at the details on the clothes, such as buttons, trimmings and stitching. Decide which of them add to the fashion appeal of the garment and add them to your drawing in pencil or coloured pencil.

Finishing off

Now draw in the arms, legs, hands and feet, and add any accessories such as hats, bags, gloves, or jewellery. Draw the shape of the accessory in pencil, then apply solid colour. Finally, add details in line, such as patterns on tights, buckles on bags and so on.

Developing a style

Once you have learned the basics of fashion drawing, you can experiment with different techniques until you find a style which suits you. On the next 12 pages you can find out how to use different media to produce various distinctive styles of fashion drawing.

41

Watercolour and pastel

This style of fashion illustration combines realistic figure drawing with casual clothes done in a soft, sketchy style, using watercolours and artist's pastels. It is a good technique to start with, as the sketchiness helps to disguise any mistakes you make.

Materials

For the life drawing: a soft lead pencil (6, 7 or 8B) or a black chinagraph pencil; a thick black artist's pastel; some A2 layout paper; a drawing board and bulldog clip and a putty rubber.

For the fashion drawing: a sheet of A2 watercolour paper (lightweight paper will need stretching* before you use it); one thick, two medium and two fine paint brushes; watercolour paints; a jam jar of water; a palette; coloured artist's pastels and a chinagraph pencil or soft lead pencil.

For optional patterns: wax crayons or masking tape.

Life drawing

Sketch on layout paper

Sketch** a friend in various poses. Work in soft pencil or chinagraph on layout paper, adding shadows in pastel, as shown above.

Now trace your best sketch on to another sheet of layout paper, adapting the clothes, if necessary, to add fashion appeal.

Tracing

Tracing on watercolour paper

Tape the drawing on to a light surface (such as a light box). Then use a 6B pencil to trace it lightly on to a sheet of watercolour paper. Simplify the lines as you trace it, and keep the drawing as clean as possible. Do not add detail and shadow at this stage.

Painting

For areas of your drawing where you want a soft-edged watercolour finish, dampen the paper with a large, clean paint brush, so that the paint flows over it evenly. For areas of hard-edged colour, paint straight on to dry paper.

Before you start painting, decide whether you will be using either of the pattern techniques shown opposite to decorate any of the garments in your picture. Do not paint any areas which you will later want to decorate using one of these methods.

1. Mix some watercolour paint with a little water in your palette. For a wider variety of shades, try mixing several colours together. Make sure you mix enough watercolour paint for all the areas you want to cover.

2. Now use your medium size paint brush to fill in any large areas of colour. Work each stroke into the last one so the paint merges and no brush strokes can be seen when you have finished.

3. Fill in medium-sized areas of the clothes, such as the skirt and hair, using the medium brushes. Then paint the small areas, such as the scarf and socks, using the finest ones.

4. Add darker tones of paint while the paper is still damp to create soft shadows (you can refer to your original life drawing to position them correctly).

* You can see how to stretch paper on page 35.
** You can find out more about poses and composition on page 40.

Adding pattern

Below are two effective techniques for making patterns on the clothes.

Wax crayon: draw a simple, abstract pattern in wax crayon on one or more of the garments in your picture. Then paint over it. The wax repels the paint, so the pattern shows up well when it dries.

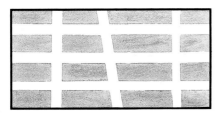

Masking tape: For hard-edged white patterns, such as stripes or checks, cut strips of masking tape and stick them down, so that they follow the contours of the body. Paint over the tape, and carefully peel it off when the paint is dry.

Adding detail

1. When the paint is dry, use coloured artist's pastels to add details, such as the woolly effect on the mini skirt, the pattern on the scarf and the face, features and hair. To get a soft, smudgy effect, apply the pastel with your finger or a cotton bud.

2. Finally, use a 6B pencil or chinagraph to add definition to your painting. You should still be able to see your original tracing lines faintly through the paint, and you can use these for reference.

Inks and markers

Here you can find out how to do a fashion illustration in a loose, impressionist style.

Materials

For sketching: a soft pencil (6, 7 or 8B) and some A2 layout paper.

For adding line and tone: a black fine-nib marker, some coloured broad-nib markers (including a flesh tone and a light grey) and some A2 cartridge paper*.

For adding texture: Letratone film (see page 33) to simulate any special textures, such as jersey or rubber.

For adding colour: one fine and one medium paint brush and some coloured drawing inks.

Preparation

Ask a friend to pose for you, in sporty or casual clothes.

Sketching

Roughly sketch your figure, as shown. If your model does not have the right clothes, choose a magazine photograph featuring appropriate garments. Ask your friend to adopt the same pose. Sketch the basic figure from life, then add clothes from the photograph.

Adding line and tone

1. Tape your sketch down on a pale surface, such as a light box**. Then tape a sheet of cartridge paper on top of it.

2. Take a black fine-nib marker and trace the outline of your sketch on to the cartridge paper. Then add the hair and face and the important features of the clothes (in this case, the main seams, hood, ribbing and boots). You can also refine the background at this stage. The pencil square in the sketch is simplified here to a single line.

3. Now fill in the face and hands using your flesh-coloured marker.

4. With your grey marker, add shadows to the figure's face and clothes.

Adding texture

Cut out pieces of **Letratone** film to fit roughly into any areas of your drawing where you want to simulate a particular texture. Peel off the backing and stick them in place.

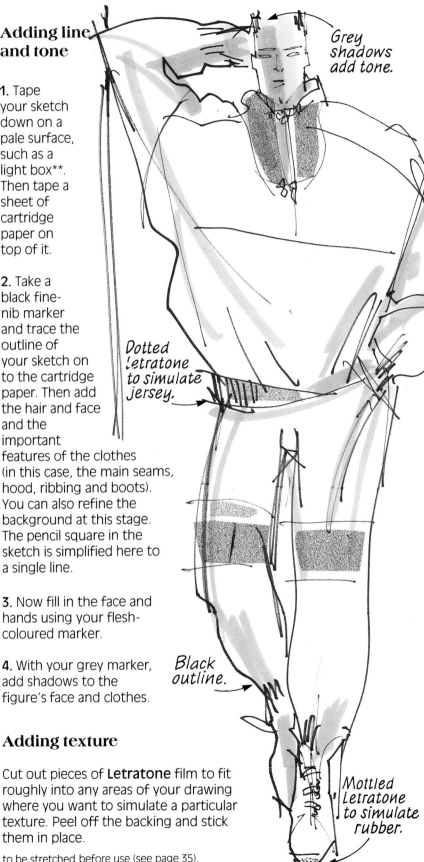

Grey shadows add tone.

Dotted Letratone to simulate jersey.

Black outline.

Mottled Letratone to simulate rubber.

* Lightweight cartridge paper will need to be stretched before use (see page 35).
** You can find out how to make a light box on page 35.

Adding colour

1. Using the wider of your two paint brushes, dipped in coloured drawing ink, fill in the areas of your illustration which you want in that colour. Use bold, confident brush strokes. Let the ink dry*.

2. If you want to colour different garments, or different parts of one garment, in contrasting coloured inks, rinse out your brush in water and apply the second colour in the same way as the first. Carry on in this way until all the larger areas of your illustration are filled in.

3. With your fine paint brush, dipped in coloured drawing ink, fill in any small details of your illustration, such as the coloured flashes on the boots.

4. If you like you can add one or two flashes of colour around the edge of the figure, to give a suggestion of background and movement. Use colours which pick out the shades in the garments.

Drawing accessories

A detailed close-up of an accessory, such as a boot or belt, can add interest to your drawing and gives you the opportunity to use a wider variety of textures. Sketch your accessory in pencil first. Then trace it off in fine black marker and add shadow using grey marker. Now add texture using Letratone, as for the clothes. Finally, add flashes of colour with your fine paint brush.

Coloured drawing inks.

Coloured flashes suggest background and movement.

* This will take 15-20 minutes.

45

Gouache

Here you can find out how to do a *graphic* style of fashion illustration using gouache. The vivid effect is achieved by applying *flat colour*. You can see how to do this opposite. It is best to attempt this style when you are confident of your figure drawing skills, as your pencil outline needs to be strong, clean and boldly drawn.

Materials

Several sheets of A3 layout paper and one sheet of stretched* A3 cartridge paper, a sharp 4H pencil, a putty rubber, one fine and one fine to medium paint brush (sizes 0 and 3 would be suitable), a selection of gouache paints, a palette, a jam jar of water and a small piece of sponge (see page 34).

Preparation

Ask a friend, or two friends, to pose for you, wearing the clothes you want to draw. If you cannot find willing models, you could use a good, clear photograph to draw from instead. Plan the composition of your illustration on a piece of rough paper, including any background objects (such as the palm tree and swimming pool in the picture shown on the opposite page). You can find out more about composition on page 40.

Drawing

Using your composition plan as a rough guide and your models (or photograph) for detailed reference, carefully draw your subjects in pencil on the sheet of stretched paper.

Try to use clean, confident pencil lines, rather than rough, sketchy ones to draw the outlines. Don't press too hard – keep the pressure on the paper light, but firm. If you make any mistakes, rub them out and draw that part again.

Applying flat colour

In the finished picture opposite, there are some areas of *flat colour*. This means they have no texture or detail. Apply flat colour to your illustration following the instructions below.

1. Plan your colour scheme.

2. Squeeze some paint into your palette and mix it with water until it is the consistency of thick cream.

3. With your fine to medium paint brush, carefully fill in any large areas of your drawing which you want to be that colour.

4. Wash out your brush and add the next colour (waiting for the first colour to dry if the areas are next to each other). Continue in the same way until you have filled in all the large areas of flat colour.

5. Fill in the smaller areas, using your fine paint brush.

Adding detail

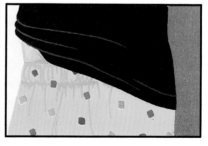

1. Using your fine paint brush, carefully paint any patterns on the clothes.

2. With the tip of the brush and a contrasting colour, add fine lines to represent any folds in the fabric.

* You can find out how to stretch paper on page 35.

Painting skin tone

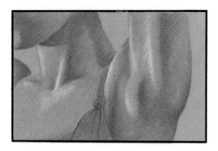

1. Use your fine to medium brush to paint a flat flesh colour all over the skin areas. If your models have different skin colours, as here, paint each one separately.

2. When this is dry, use your fine brush to add shading in a slightly darker colour wherever you want to give the impression of shadows or hollows on your figure's skin (for example, under the arms and around the neck).

3. Now use a light flesh colour to add highlights where the light catches the model's skin (for example, on the cheek).

Adding texture

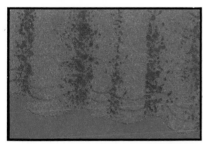

To get a textured effect, like that on the towel, use a small piece of sponge to dab a darker shade of the background colour gently over the flat colour. Apply the darker shade in lines, to give the impression of folds in the fabric.

Collage

Collage is one of the most exciting methods of creating a fashion illustration. A collage done for fun or for your *portfolio* can include as many different layers and unusual textures as you like (see below). You may be more restricted in what you can use in a collage commissioned for publication. This is due to the difficulty of reproducing certain textures when printed.

Materials

For the sketch: several sheets of A2 layout paper, a soft pencil (6, 7 or 8B) and a putty rubber.

For the collage: a sheet of heavyweight A2 cartridge paper; several sheets of coloured paper (such as cover paper) and other optional collage materials (see below); a scalpel; a large piece of hardboard for cutting on; some spray-on glue; a pair of scissors; one light coloured and one dark coloured oil pastel.

Alternative media

The collage on the right is made from coloured paper, which is a simple and versatile material. Once you have learned the technique, however, you may want to experiment with other media. Below are some suggestions.

Photocopied fabric can be used for simulating different textures. You can have photocopies made at instant print shops and libraries.

Magazine clippings, whether abstract patterns or photographs of objects, such as jewellery and handbags can provide interest in collages.

Tissue paper comes in many colours and can be crumpled, decorated with paint or pastel, or used in several layers to create different effects.

Outline

Working from a live model or a photograph, roughly sketch your figure in soft pencil on layout paper. Then trace the outline of the figure and the simplified shape of the garments on to your sheet of cartridge paper using a light box*.

Rough sketch on layout paper.

Planning the collage

Collage pieces assembled on cartridge paper.

1. Plan your colour scheme. Then put each sheet of coloured paper in turn on the hardboard and lay your sketch on top. Using the sketch as a *template* (guide), roughly cut out with a scalpel the shape of each part of your drawing, in the appropriate colours.

* You can find out how to make a light box on page 35.

2. Now discard the cut layout paper and assemble all the collage pieces on the cartridge paper you prepared earlier.

Background

Before you stick the collage pieces down, try cutting out (or even tearing) an abstract background shape in a complementary colour, and slot it in behind the collage pieces. This can add impact to your illustration.

Sticking it down

When you are satisfied with the arrangement of the pieces, spray the back of each one in turn with glue* and stick it carefully in position. Start with the biggest pieces (such as the background shape and the main items of clothing) which form the basis of the collage. Then move on to the smaller ones, overlapping them where necessary.

Adding detail

Once you have the basic shape of the collage stuck down, you can add smaller details, still using cut paper, such as the lips and button in the illustration on the left. You do not need to use a template for these. You can simply draw the shapes on coloured paper and cut them out with scissors. If you wanted to add any accessories cut from magazine photographs, such as a pair of sun glasses or a belt, you could add them at this stage. If you do this, make sure that they are in proportion with the rest of your collage.

Adding definition

Finally, use pastel to add definition to your collage. Using a dark colour, re-draw the garment shapes, sketchily, just inside the edges of the collage pieces. Emphasize the important details (in this case the stitching on the lapels and the shape of the cuffs). Still in a dark shade, carefully draw in the features of the face, keeping them simple and bold. Then, with a light coloured pastel, add *highlights* where appropriate (in the hair, for example).

* Follow the instructions on the can carefully.

Pastel and pencil

Not all fashion illustrations feature clothes. Make-up, accessories and jewellery are common subjects too. A close-up, head-and-shoulders view of your model is best for this type of fashion drawing.

On these two pages the main subject of the drawing is the hair, and the artist has worked in shades of black and grey to give a striking effect. To emphasize the make-up, you could use the same materials, but introduce colour.

Materials

Several sheets of A3 layout paper; a soft pencil (6B, 7B or 8B); a sheet of lightweight watercolour paper, either NOT* or H.P.*, depending on your preference; some oil pastels; a small can of petroleum-based spirit for softening the pastel; some paper tissues for spreading the pastel; some water-soluble crayons; some pencil crayons and some fixative.

Preparation

If possible, ask a friend to pose for you. Otherwise, choose a good head-and-shoulders photograph to work from, which features strong make-up, interesting jewellery or an unusual hairstyle.

Rough line drawing

Make several quick line drawings of your subject, using black pastel or soft pencil on layout paper. Do not overwork the drawings. If you get the proportions wrong, start again on a fresh piece of paper. You can find out how to draw heads in proportion on page 38. Choose the rough you like best and trace it on to another sheet of layout paper. Then develop it, adding more detail until you have a good basic guide to use for your final drawing.

Now tape your line drawing on to a light box** (this is essential, as the watercolour paper is too thick to see through otherwise). Lay the watercolour paper over the top.

Shading

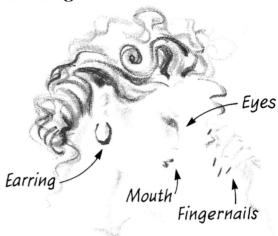

Eyes

Earring

Mouth

Fingernails

Using your line drawing as a guide, shade in the hair, face and shoulders, using the edge of a small piece of light-coloured pastel. Use a darker shade to mark the eyes and mouth, define the hair and position details such as the earrings and fingernails.

Adding line

Now take a dark-coloured pencil crayon and trace the outline of your drawing from the rough, on to the watercolour paper. Keep the line flowing as you draw. To stop your hand from smudging the pastel as you work, put a scrap of paper between it and the drawing.

* You can find out what these terms mean on page 33.
   ** You can see how to make a light box on page 35.

Adding tone and definition

Now use a coloured pastel crayon (or, in this case, a mid-grey) to add tone and depth to the hair, using bold, upwards and outwards strokes to give your drawing movement and vitality. Add a little dark-coloured pastel to the lips, nails and earrings to give them greater definition. Then strengthen the outline in areas such as the neck, shoulders and particularly in the hair, using a water-soluble crayon.

Adding background

Use the side of a small piece of oil pastel to shade thickly and evenly around the edge of your drawing, leaving a narrow white band (or halo) between the drawing and the background. This prevents it from looking too heavy. Dampen some tissues with petrol and wipe them gently over the pastel to soften it and spread it evenly. Finally, spray fixative on to your drawing, to prevent smudging.

51

Mixed media

Here you can find out how to use a variety of media to produce a rich, detailed style of fashion illustration which is particularly good for conveying texture and volume in fabric. The proportions and features of the figure are slightly exaggerated to add impact to the illustration.

Materials

A few sheets of layout paper; a sheet of cartridge or H.P.* watercolour paper (stretched**, if lightweight); a soft pencil (6B, 7B or 8B); a putty rubber; a drawing board and bulldog clip; some watercolour paints; a palette; a jam jar of water; a smudger; oil pastels; gouache; drawing inks; two or three fine to medium size brushes (such as sizes 3, 4 and 6); a wide, bristle brush (at least size 14) and a small can of petroleum-based spirit.

Preparation

Draw a few quick thumbnail sketches in pencil on layout paper to work out the pose and composition of your drawing. Choose the one you like best, and ask a friend to adopt the same pose for you to draw from.

Outline

Using your model for reference, begin by drawing a faint outline of the figure in soft pencil on your piece of cartridge or watercolour paper. This is just a rough guide to use as a starting point for your illustration and you should be prepared to change and refine it later, as your work progresses.

Applying the base colour

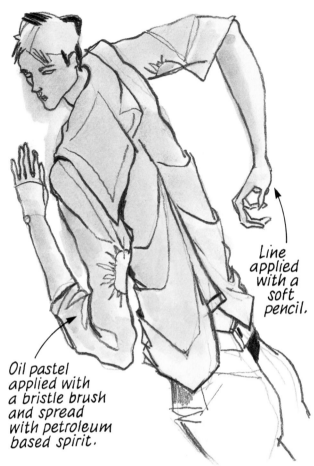

Line applied with a soft pencil.

Oil pastel applied with a bristle brush and spread with petroleum based spirit.

Using your bristle brush dipped in pastel, apply colour roughly to all the main areas of your drawing, such as the clothes, limbs, face and so on.

As you apply each colour, dip your brush in a little petroleum-based spirit and brush it over the layer of pastel you have just put down, to spread it evenly on the paper. Give your model a break while you leave it to dry.

Definition with colour and line

Now you can go on to define your figure, using pencil and whatever combination of coloured media you like (see the list of materials on the left for some suggestions). Ask your model to adopt the same pose as before, and keep glancing at him/her continually, while you add definition as shown on the next page.

* You can find out what this term means on page 33.
** You can find out how to stretch paper on page 35.

1. Start to work down your figure adding line with a soft pencil, and colour where you need it, as you go along. Resist the temptation to draw a pencil outline and then fill it in, as this will result in too rigid a style.

2. If using oil pastel, you can spread it on the paper as you did for the base colour. If you use watercolour, gouache or drawing inks on top of oil pastel, you will get an interesting effect, as the oil and water-based media mingle. If you want to use artist's pastels, rather than oil pastels, with paint or inks, apply the wet media first. Then let them dry and add the pastel on top.

Adding tone and texture

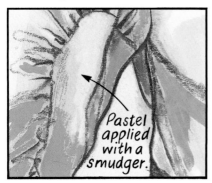

Pastel applied with a smudger.

Now go on to add tone and texture to your drawing, starting with the details of the clothes. Use a smudger or fine paint brush, dipped in oil pastel and white spirit, to draw in folds and shadows (for example, in the illustration on the right, the elbow patches and folds down the back of the shirt were done in this way). Then move on to smaller areas, such as the face, adding tone around the eyes and nose, under the chin and beneath the ear, to give an impression of shadows.

Finishing off

Finally, stand a little way away from your illustration and look at it through half-closed eyes to check any imbalance in the amount of detail in different areas. Add a bit more line to strengthen the areas which need it. Do not *overwork* your illustration. Once you start wondering whether to add a bit more, it is probably the best time to stop.

Mounting and presentation

Whether you do fashion illustration as a hobby or a career, your work will look more impressive if you present it well. You can find out how on these two pages.

Why mount your illustrations?

Mounting your illustrations protects them and makes them look neat and tidy.

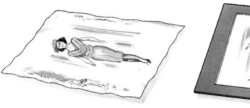

This unmounted fashion illustration is creased around the edges and looks untidy.

Trimmed and mounted on card, the illustration looks much more professional.

Choosing a border

For a plain border, use white card or a coloured card which goes well with your illustration. If you prefer a decorative border, you could cover the card with a stylish wrapping paper, paint a pattern on it, or make a collage design. Try to ensure that the pattern does not overpower your illustration.

Positioning your illustration

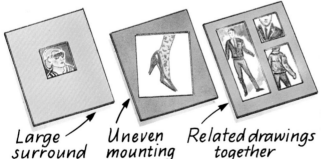

Large surround

Uneven mounting

Related drawings together

The position of your illustration on its mount can also enhance its effect. It does not always have to be mounted evenly in the centre. Sometimes an unusual layout shows it off best.

How to mount your illustrations

There are two main types of mount. A **window mount** is a piece of card with a hole (window) in it, behind which the illustration is displayed. A **flat mount** is a piece of card glued to the back of your illustration. You can see how to make them below.

1. Window mounting

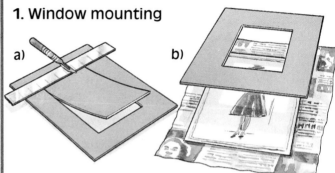

a)

b)

Try out various shapes and sizes of window, using scrap paper. Draw the one which works best on a piece of card. Then cut it out using a scalpel and steel ruler.

Cover the picture area of your illustration with a piece of scrap paper to protect it. Then spray glue* carefully around the edges. Stick the mount firmly in position.

2. Flat mounting

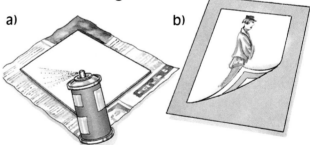

a)

b)

If you want a border round your drawing, use a piece of card which is bigger than it. Spray glue* evenly over the back of your illustration, then stick it on to the mount.

If you prefer, you can use double-sided tape. Stick tape along the edges of the back of your illustration. Peel off the tape backing and stick the illustration to your mount.

* You can find out more about spray-on glue on page 34.

Protecting your work

Once you have mounted your illustrations, you could put them in a *portfolio* to keep them clean and tidy. Alternatively, you could keep them in transparent covers (see the box below).

What is a portfolio?

A portfolio is a large flat case for keeping your illustrations in. The zip-fastening ones made from plastic or leather often have ring binders, with detachable plastic wallets which are ideal for protecting your work. You can keep two illustrations, back to back, in each wallet.

You can also buy cheaper plastic or card portfolios where the illustrations are kept loose inside. If you choose this type, it is a good idea to cover your illustrations with *acetate*, or have them *laminated.* You can find out how to do this at the bottom of the page.

As well as keeping your work clean and tidy, most portfolios have handles, so you can carry them around. This is useful if you are going to a college interview, or to see prospective clients to find professional work in fashion illustration.

Portfolio

Drawings in plastic wallets

Ring binder

Mounts same size as wallets to keep drawings upright.

Zip fastener

Organizing your portfolio

Arrange the work in your portfolio so it looks as interesting as possible. You do not need to keep your illustrations in subject areas (men's wear, women's wear and so on).

For a college interview, it is best to show a wide range of different styles and techniques throughout. If you are looking for work, only show what you do best or what you think will be most suitable.

Transparent covers

If you want to display your illustrations on your wall or at an exhibition, or if you have the type of portfolio which does not have plastic wallets inside, it is a good idea to cover each one with a layer of transparent film to keep it clean. There are two ways you can do this.

1. Acetate

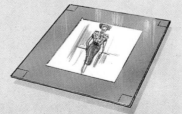

Cut the *acetate** to the size of your mount, then tack it on with a small piece of clear tape at each corner.

2. Lamination

Most photocopying shops will *laminate* illustrations for you. To do this, they seal them in plastic.

---

* You can buy acetate from art shops.

Finding work as a fashion illustrator

Most fashion illustrators work *freelance*. This means that they find work with different companies. If you work freelance, your time is your own, which gives you freedom. However, organizing your work can be hard to get used to.

On these two pages you can find out about the types of freelance work available, and how to find it.

Magazines

Most fashion magazines use some fashion illustrations.* Find as much magazine work as you can at first: it is a good showcase for your work, and will help you to become established as an illustrator.

Newspapers

Newspapers often use illustrations in their fashion reports (which usually appear weekly). This is because a strong, simple illustration often reproduces better than a photograph in black and white.

Advertising

Advertising agencies handling accounts for companies who make clothes, cosmetics, accessories and so on, may use fashion illustrations in press advertisements and on hoardings. Advertising work usually pays well.

Packaging

Some companies use illustrations to decorate boxes and wrappers for their goods. Approach companies who make cosmetics, tights, or anything which is packaged in a fashion-conscious way.

Fashion forecasting

Fashion forecasting magazines predict what trends will be in future seasons, as a guide for people in the fashion industry. The fashions are seldom available to be photographed, so they use illustrations instead.

Dress patterns

Companies which produce dressmaking patterns use fashion illustrations on pattern envelopes and in catalogues. For this type of work, a simple style of illustration is required, to give the garment a wide appeal.

Chainstores

Many of the big chainstores have their own art departments, producing advertisements, catalogues and display material. They sometimes use fashion illustrators for this type of work.

56

* French and Italian magazines tend to use more illustrations than other countries.

Making contacts

When your *portfolio* is ready, ring up different companies in the fields mentioned on the opposite page. Make as many appointments as you can to show your work.

If you are ringing a magazine or newspaper, ask to speak to the art editor. If it is a large company, such as a chainstore or advertising agency, ask to speak to the person in charge of the art department. Find out their name from the receptionist.

When you get through to the right person, tell them your name, that you are a fashion illustrator, and that you would like to show them your portfolio. If they are too busy to see you, send them some photocopies of your work and a business card (see right). If they want to see you, note the date and time of the appointment and the person's name. Be sure to turn up on time.

If you can give a very brief description of each piece in your portfolio, saying why you did it and the effect you wanted to achieve, this will create a good impression.

Stages in a job

If you are lucky, some of the contacts you make may eventually ask you to do jobs for them. Below you can see the stages involved in completing a job.

1. Commission. This is when someone asks you to do a job. They will **brief** you (tell you what they want) and usually give you a purchase order, giving the name of the job, the fee and the *deadline* (delivery date).

2. Delivery. This is when you take the completed work back to the person who commissioned it.

They may ask you to make **corrections** to the job within a certain time. You don't usually get any extra money.

3. Acceptance/rejection. When they have seen your completed job, the person who commissioned it will usually accept it. If they are unhappy with it, they may pay you a rejection fee (usually 50% of the agreed fee for the job).

4. Payment. To receive payment you usually have to send an invoice (or bill) to the company's accounts department.

Business cards

Name, address and telephone number

You can have business cards printed, or, if you can't afford this, design your own and photocopy it. Give a card to a prospective client as a reminder, when you leave.

Managing your money*

It is a good idea to ask your bank manager for advice about managing money. He or she may offer you a bank loan to pay for things like your portfolio, printing your business cards and perhaps buying an answerphone.

Sidelines

Fashion illustration work can be hard to find, even if you follow all the tips on this page. It is a good idea to have another skill to rely on for the times when work is slack. Experienced illustrators sometimes find part-time teaching work.

If you have done a course which included either fashion design or graphic design, you could look for work in those areas too.

57

* See the **Usborne Introduction to Business** (details on page 62)

About fabrics

A basic understanding of how fabrics are made and what properties they have is essential if you are considering a career in fashion design. Many things will govern your choice of fabric for a garment, or collection. First you should take into account the weight, cost and practicality of a fabric. Only then should the more enjoyable choice of colour, pattern and texture be made. Here you can find out about the main variables in fabric production. If you do a course in fashion design, you will learn about fabrics in greater depth.

How fabrics are made

Most fabrics are made in one of four ways: by weaving, knitting, twisting together threads of spun fibre or by bonding the fibres. Here you can see the pattern of the yarns in the first three manufacturing methods. Bonded fabrics (such as felt) do not have a clearly identifiable pattern.

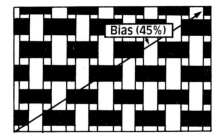

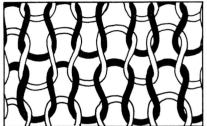

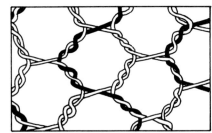

Woven fabrics consist of vertical and horizontal threads called warp and weft which interlock at right angles. Woven fabrics are firm, but have little stretch, except when they are cut on the bias.

Knitted fabrics consist of interlocking loops of yarn in rows. They can be produced as flat lengths or tubes of fabric depending on the machine used. Knitted fabrics are stretchy, and can ladder easily.

Lace or net fabrics are made by machines which twist yarns around each other. The number and pattern of twists determines the texture and design. Lace is usually loose in structure, so it is often see-through.

Cost

The cost of a fabric depends on the availability of the raw materials used to make it and on the number and complexity of the processes involved in its manufacture. Silk, for example, is a comparatively rare and luxurious fabric because the yarn used to make it is produced by silk worms and has to be unwound laboriously from their cocoons. Generally, natural fabrics such as silk, cotton, linen and wool are more expensive than synthetic ones, such as viscose, polyester and acrylic. Synthetic fabrics and mixtures of synthetic and natural fabrics are often used by *mass market* designers to keep costs down. *Couturiers* and top designers use natural fabrics a lot because they need not be so cost-conscious. The chart on the next page shows the comparative cost of some of the most commonly used fabrics.

Weight

The weight of a fabric depends on the natural properties and thickness of the yarn used to make it, and on the method of manufacture. Cotton, for example, can be made into fine lawn for summer dresses, or corduroy for winter coats. Wool is traditionally used for winter garments, as it is a warm fabric, but it can also be produced in lightweight forms, such as flannel. Most synthetic fabrics come in several different weights and can be substituted for their natural equivalents. For example, viscose and acrylic are often used instead of wool.

Finish

Variations in the finish (surface texture) of a fabric may be introduced at several stages. The yarn may vary in thickness, creating random patterns when woven or knitted; the weaving or knitting process may be varied to produce different textures; or the fabric may be treated after it is woven or knitted to produce a special effect. The finish of a fabric affects its look, its weight and the way it falls.

Colour and pattern

Colour can be introduced into fabric in three ways. The yarn can be dyed before the fabric is made; the fabric can be dyed; a pattern can be printed on to the fabric. Many different patterns can be achieved by weaving or knitting using different coloured yarns. Machines can produce regular patterns, such as checks, stripes and zig-zags. However, abstract or very complex floral designs have to be printed.

Properties of common fabrics

Fabric	Composition	Weight	Finish	Cost	Uses
Calico	Cotton	Depends on quality, but usually fairly light.	Smooth, dull. May be opaque, depending on quality.	Very cheap	Summer dresses, bedding, *couturiers' toiles*
Chiffon	Silk, nylon or polyester	Very light	Fine, open structure. Translucent.	Silk chiffon is expensive. Synthetic chiffons cost less.	Scarves, evening wear (mainly for decoration).
Corduroy	Cotton or rayon	Fairly heavy. Depends on depth of pile.	Has pile. Soft, ridged surface.	Fairly expensive.	Hardwearing indoor and outdoor garments.
Denim	Cotton or polyester/cotton and stretch types	Heavy	Dense, dull, slightly rough	Cheap	Hardwearing clothes, particularly jeans and jackets
Flannel	Wool or wool/cotton	Medium to light	Very smooth and soft. Has a slightly raised surface.	All-wool flannel is quite expensive	Lightweight suits, jackets and skirts
Gaberdine	Wool, cotton, rayon	Medium	Dense, dull with a diagonal weave on the front	Fairly expensive	Mainly rainwear. Also dresses and suits.
Grosgrain	Originally silk. Now available in rayon and acetate.	Medium	Dense, lustrous with prominent ridges woven in.	Fairly expensive	Evening wear
Jersey	Anything which may be knitted, such as wool, cotton, acrylic	Various	Usually fairly loose, smooth and soft	Cheap	Underwear, leisure wear, knitwear, sports wear
Poplin	Cotton or rayon	Light to medium	Smooth, dense, with fine ridges woven in.	Fairly cheap	Shirts, dresses, pyjamas etc
Satin	Silk	Medium to heavy	Dense, smooth, lustrous	Very expensive	Evening wear
Seersucker	Cotton	Light	Puckered surface, usually in ridges	Fairly cheap	Summer dresses, blouses; lingerie
Taffeta	Originally silk, but now more often synthetic	Medium to heavy	Dense, lustrous; smooth or very faintly ribbed	Synthetic versions are fairly cheap.	Evening wear, petticoats, lining
Tweed	Mainly wool. Synthetic imitations also available.	Medium to heavy	Rough, bobbly, fairly loose weave	Expensive	Suits, skirts, coats
Velvet	Silk, cotton, rayon, nylon	Medium to heavy	Very dense. Thick, soft pile.	Expensive	Evening wear, skirts, coats, suits

Careers in fashion

Jobs in fashion range from glamorous, high profile work, such as modelling, to behind-the-scenes skills, such as pattern-cutting. For some careers, professional qualifications are a must; for others, experience and enthusiasm count for more. Here, you can find out about some popular jobs in the fashion world.

Fashion designer

Description: designing clothes (see pages 10-13).

Qualifications: various degree and diploma courses available (see pages 62-63).

Personal qualities: love of fashion, imagination, an eye for colour and detail, technical skills, artistic sense.

Getting there: build up a portfolio of fashion illustrations* (see page 55) and apply for a place on a fashion design course (see pages 62-63 for addresses).

Textile designer

Description: designing fabric weaves and prints for clothes and furnishings.

Qualifications: specialist degree and diploma courses available (see pages 62-63). Also taught as part of some fashion design courses.

Personal qualities: artistic flair, colour sense, technical skill and an eye for detail.

Getting started: build up a collection of fabric designs on paper. Apply for courses in textiles and/or fashion design.

Fashion illustrator

Description: drawing and painting clothes for commercial use (see pages 56-57).

Qualifications: few courses teach fashion illustration alone. It is included in some fashion design courses.

Personal qualities: artistic flair, love of fashion, self-discipline.

Getting started: practise drawing until you have a number of good illustrations in your *portfolio*, then apply for a course or try to work on a freelance basis.

Pattern cutter

Description: drawing out and sizing paper patterns for fashion designers or clothing manufacturers (you can find out more about this on page 13).

Qualifications: formal training is absolutely essential. Diploma courses are available at a number of colleges. Pattern cutting is also taught as part of most fashion design diploma and degree courses.

Personal qualities: fashion sense, patience, dexterity and a good eye for detail.

Getting started: apply for a place on a course in either pattern cutting or fashion design.

Teacher of fashion design or illustration

Description: teaching students of fashion design, fashion illustration or both at degree or diploma level or at evening classes.

Qualifications: degree or diploma in fashion design and experience in the fashion industry.

Personal qualities: artistic flair, love of fashion and awareness of its trends, enthusiasm, patience and the ability to communicate.

Getting there: maintain contacts in fashion education while acquiring commercial experience. Start by teaching part-time.

Fashion photographer

Description: photographing clothes on fashion models for use in newspapers, magazines or advertisements.

Qualifications: degree and diploma courses available, but not essential.

Personal qualities: artistic flair, an eye for colour, detail and composition, and a lively, outgoing personality.

Getting there: apply for photography courses or a job as an assistant to an established photographer (not necessarily in fashion photography – general experience is also useful). Build up a portfolio of your best fashion shots.

60   * Applicants are not expected to have done any actual fashion design before going to college.

Fashion journalist

Description: writing fashion articles for newspapers and magazines.

Qualifications: some experience of journalism is useful. Degree and diploma courses are available in journalism, media and communications. A number of fashion courses also have fashion journalism options.

Personal qualities: a good writing style, an interest in fashion, tenacity, enthusiasm and the ability to research a subject extremely thoroughly.

Getting started: apply for courses in journalism or gain reporting experience by getting a job in mainstream journalism.

Public relations consultant

Description: providing publicity and information about fashion designers, manufacturers and retailers to the press and potential customers.

Qualifications: these are not essential. Some business studies courses include public relations as an option.

Personal qualities: business sense, good communication skills, tact, dynamism and initiative.

Getting there: apply for courses in public relations or business studies courses which offer public relations as part of the training. Alternatively, apply for any kind of job with a public relations company to get experience.

Fashion model

Description: modelling clothes for photographs or at fashion shows.

Qualifications: none. Some modelling courses teach grooming and deportment, but unless you have the looks and figure for it, training is a waste of time.

Personal qualities: figure, looks and age are the essential factors. Modelling is a short-lived career. The earlier you start, the better your chances. Only the most famous and successful models go on working into their thirties. As well as having good looks, models need patience, good humour, energy and the ability to communicate.

Boys must be at least 5′ 10″ tall, with a medium build (neither fat nor thin) and good looks. They must start their modelling careers between the ages of 16 and 22.

Girls must be between 5′ 8″ and 5′ 10″ tall and must take size 10* or 12** clothes. Good looks and clear skin are essential. Well-cut hair and good fingernails are an asset. Girls must start modelling between the ages of 16 and 20.

Getting there: send a good, clear, full-length photograph and a close-up head and shoulders shot of yourself to some reputable modelling agencies. Write your name, age, height and size on the back, and enclose a stamped, self-addressed envelope.

Fashion buyer

Description: responsible for ordering stocks of clothes for shops, especially the larger chain stores.

Qualifications: none essential. Some business schools run courses on retailing which cover buying.

Personal qualities: an interest in fashion, a strong colour sense and an eye for detail; a good business sense, initiative.

Getting there: a degree in any subject is a basic requirement of most retailers who are recruiting buying trainees. Business studies which include retailing would be especially useful.

Stylist

Description: co-ordinating the clothes, jewellery, accessories and so on, used in fashion photographs and catwalk shows.

Qualifications: none. Most stylists move into styling via other fashion careers, such as designing.

Personal qualities: love of fashion, a very good colour sense, an eye for detail, energy and diplomacy.

Getting there: build up a portfolio of fashion shots which you have styled. You may get the chance to do this by working as an assistant to an established stylist, or photographer.

* European size 38, US size 8
** European size 40, US size 10

Going further

If you would like to find out more about any aspect of fashion, the books and selected courses listed on these two pages will give you a good starting point.

Book list

Fashion: general

Couture: The Great Fashion Designers
Caroline Rennolds Milbank
Thames & Hudson
(published in the USA under the imprint Stewart, Tabori & Chang)

Karl Lagerfeld: A Fashion Journal
Anna Piagi
Thames & Hudson
(published in the USA under the imprint Weidenfeld & Nicholson)

Seasons
Bruce Oldfield
Pan Books

The Encyclopaedia of Fashion
Georgina O'Hara
Thames & Hudson
(published in the USA under the imprint Abrams)

Yves Saint Laurent
Yves Saint Laurent et al
Thames & Hudson
(published in the USA under the imprint Clarkson Potter)

Fashion design

Encyclopedia of Fashion Details
Patrick John Ireland
Batsford

Erté Fashion Designs
Erté
Dover

Fashion Design and Illustration I
John M. Turnpenny
Hutchison

Fashion Design Drawing and Presentation
Patrick John Ireland
Batsford

History of fashion

Adorned in Dreams: Fashion and Modernity
Elizabeth Wilson
Virago
(published in the USA under the imprint University of California Press)

A History of Fashion
J. Anderson Black & Madge Garland
Orbis

Costume and Fashion: a Concise History
James Laver
Thames & Hudson
(published in the USA under the imprint Thames & Hudson Inc.)

History of 20th Century Fashion
Elizabeth Ewing
Batsford
(published in the USA under the imprint Barnes & Noble)

The History of Haute Couture 1850-1950
Diana de Marly
Batsford
(published in the USA under the imprint Holmes & Meier)

Fashion illustration

Figure Drawing for Fashion
Isao Yajima
Graphic-Sha

Fashion Drawing in Vogue
William Packer
Thames & Hudson
(published in the USA under the imprint Putnam Publishers)

Fashion Illustration in New York
Peter Sato
Graphic-sha

Fashion in Paris
From the "Journal des Dames des Modes" 1912-1913
Thames & Hudson
(published in the USA under the imprint Rizzoli Publishers)

From the Ballet Russes to Vogue
The Art of Georges Lepape
Claude Lepape & Thierry Defert
Thames & Hudson
(published in the USA under the imprint Vendome)

Business and careers

Usborne Introduction to Business
Janet Cook
Usborne Publishing

Careers in Fashion (2nd Edition)
Carole Chester
Kogan Page

Fashion courses

UK Courses

Brighton Polytechnic
Mithras House, Lewes Road
Brighton BN2 4AT.

Offers: B.A. (Hons) in Fashion Textiles with Administration

Chelsea School of Art
Manresa Road, Chelsea
London SW3 6LS.

Offers: Foundation Course* in Art and Design; B/TEC National Diploma in General Art and Design; B/TEC Higher National Diploma in Textile Design

Eastbourne College of Arts and Technology
St Anne's Road, Eastbourne
East Sussex BN21 2HS.

Offers: B/TEC National Diploma in General Vocational Design;
Dip.CSD (Chartered Society of Designers) courses in Printed Textiles, Constructed Textiles and Fashion Design

Epsom School of Art and Design
Ashley Road, Epsom
Surrey KT18 5BE.

Offers: B/TEC National Diploma in Fashion; B/TEC Higher National Diploma in Fashion Design

Harrow College of Higher Education
Northwick Park,
Harrow HA1 3TP.

Offers: B.A. (Hons) in Fashion

Kingston Polytechnic
Knights Park
Kingston-upon-Thames
Surrey KT1 2QJ.

Offers: Foundation course* in Art and Design; B.A. (Hons) Fashion

London College of Fashion
20 John Prince's Street,
Oxford Street, London W1M 0BJ.

Offers: B/TEC National Diploma in Fashion; B/TEC National Diploma in Fashion/Embroidery; B/TEC Higher National Diploma in Fashion; B/TEC National Diploma – The Business of Fashion

Medway College of Design
Fort Pitt, Rochester
Kent ME1 1DZ.

Offers: B/TEC National Diploma in Design; B/TEC Higher National Diploma in Design

Middlesex Polytechnic
Cat Hill, Barnet,
Hertfordshire EN4 8HT.

Offers: B.A. (Hons) in Printed Textiles; Constructed Textiles; Fashion Design

North East London Polytechnic
Romford Road, Stratford
London E15 4LZ.

Offers: 4 year B.A. (Hons) sandwich course in Fashion Design with Marketing

Ravensbourne College of Design and Communication
Walden Road, Chislehurst
Bromley
Kent BR7 5NS.

Offers: Foundation Course* in Fashion; B.A. Hons in Fashion Design

* Foundation courses are broadly-based and usually last for one year. They prepare school-leavers for higher education at degree or diploma level.

Royal College Of Art
Kensington Gore
London SW7 2EU.
Offers: MDes (RCA) in Fashion Design; MA (RCA) in Textile Design

Faculty of Art and Design
Southampton Institute of Higher Education
East Park Terrace
Southampton SO09 4WW.
Offers: B/TEC National Diploma in Fashion Design; B/TEC Higher National Diploma in Fashion Design; B/TEC National Certificate in Fashion

St Martin's School of Art
107 Charing Cross Road,
London WC2H 0DH.
Offers: 3 year full-time B.A. (Hons) in Fashion; 4 year sandwich B.A. (Hons) in Fashion; 2 year full-time M.A. in Fashion

Trent Polytechnic Nottingham
Burton Street
Nottingham NG1 4BU
Offers: B.A. (Hons) in Fashion; B.A. (Hons) in Textiles; B.A. (Hons) in Knitwear and Fabric Design

Winchester School of Art
Park Avenue, Winchester
Hampshire SO23 8DL.
Offers: B.A. (Hons) in Textiles/Fashion; B.A. (Hons) in Textiles/Fashion (50/50 option); B.A. (Hons) in Textiles/Fashion with extended design history studies

US Courses

Art Institute of Atlanta
3376 Peachtree Road, N.E.
Atlanta, Georgia 30326, USA.
Offers: Majors in Fashion Illustration and Fashion Merchandising

Bauder Fashion College
300 Biscayne Blvd Way
Miami, Florida 33131, USA.
Offers: Associate Degree in Fashion Design

Bauder Fashion College
3355 Lennox Road, N.E.
Atlanta, Georgia 30326, USA.
Offers: Associate Degree in Fashion Design

Cornell University
Ithaca, New York 14853
USA.
Offers: Bachelor in Textile Design

Ellsworth Community College
1100 College Ave.
Iowa Falls, Iowa 50126
USA.
Offers: Associate Degree in Fashion Design

Fashion Institute of Design and Marketing

a) 818 West 7th St
Los Angeles, California 90017
USA

b) 790 Market St
San Francisco, California 94102
USA
Both offer: Certificate and Degree courses in Fashion Design and Textile Design

Fashion Institute of Technology
227 W.27th Street
New York, NY 10001, USA.
Offers: Associate Degree in Fashion Design; Bachelor in Textile Design; Bachelor of Fine Arts (specializing in Fashion Design or Fashion and Related Industries)

French Fashion Academy
600 Madison Ave.
New York, NY 10022
USA.
Offers: Certificate in Fashion Design

Louise Salinger Academy of Fashion
101 Jessie St
San Francisco, California 94105
USA.
Offers: Associate Degree in Fashion Design

Mayer School of Fashion
64 W.36th Street
New York, NY 10018, USA.
Offers: Certificate in Fashion Design

Parsons School of Design
560 7th Avenue
New York, NY 10018
USA

Offers: Bachelor of Fine Arts in Fashion Illustration.

Philadelphia College of Textiles and Science
Philadelphia, Pennsylvania 19144
USA.
Offers: Bachelors in Textile Design

Tracey-Warner School of Fashion Design
401 N. Broad St
Philadelphia, Pennsylvania 19108
USA.
Offers: Associate Degree in Fashion Design

University of California
Davis, California 95616, USA.
Offers: Bachelor in Textile Design

Virginia Marti School of Fashion Design
11308 Detroit Ave.
Cleveland, Ohio 44102, USA.
Offers: Diploma in Fashion Design

Canadian Courses

Capilano College
2055 Purcell Way
North Vancouver
British Columbia
V7J 3H5 Canada
Offers: course in Fashion

College Lasalle
2015 rue Drummond
Montreal, Quebec
H3G 1W7 Canada.
Offers: course in Fashion Design

Fanshawe College of Applied Arts and Technology
1460 Oxford Street East
London, Ontario
N5W 5H1 Canada.
Offers: course in Fashion Design

Fraser Valley College
45600 Airport Road
Chilliwack, British Columbia
V2P 6R4 Canada.
Offers: course in Fashion Design

George Brown College of Applied Arts and Technology
Box 1015 Station B
Toronto, Ontario
M5T 2T9 Canada.
Offers: course in Creative Fashion Design

Ryerson Polytechnical Institute
350 Victoria Street
Toronto, Ontario
M5B 2K3 Canada.
Offers: Diploma in Fashion

Sheridan College of Applied Arts and Technology
Trafalgar Road
Oakville, Ontario, L6H 2L1 Canada.
Offers: course in Fashion Technique and Design

New Zealand courses

Wellington Polytechnic
Private Bag
Wellington, New Zealand.
Offers: Certificate in Clothing and Textiles; Diploma in Textile Design

Australian courses

Curtin University of Technology
Perth, Western Australia.
Offers: B.A. in Design

Riverina-Murray Institute of Higher Education
Wagga Campus
Boorooma Street, North Wagga Wagga NSW 2650, Australia.
Offers: Bachelor of Visual Arts degree in Textiles

Queensland House
Seven Hills College
Division of Technical and Further Education
59 Peel Street
South Brisbane 4101, Australia.
Offers: B.A. in Fashion; B.A. in Textile Design

Sydney College of the Arts
P.O. Box 226
Glebe 2037, Sydney, Australia.
Offers: B.A. in Fashion and Textile Design

Glossary

Acetate: clear plastic film.

Adding line: in figure drawing, using pencil to outline torso and limbs, and position features.

Block: a master pattern from which others can be adapted.

Blocking in: in figure drawing, shading in the model's shape.

Brief: concise instructions, provided for a particular piece of work, which must be followed precisely.

Bustle: a pad worn under a long, full skirt, attached to the back below waist level, to emphasize the hips.

Buyer: *see* fashion buyer.

Catwalk: a raised platform used to present a fashion show.

Centre back: line running through the centre of a figure.

Centre front (CF): line running through the centre of a figure, parallel to the backbone.

Cockle: a wrinkle or pucker in a sheet of paper.

Collage: an illustration made of layers of coloured paper and other materials.

Collection: a range of co-ordinated clothes.

Colourways: the choice of alternative colours or colour combinations for a garment.

Composition: in figure drawing, the pose and position of a figure on the page.

Construction marks: in figure drawing, marks made to show the position of features and the angles of the body.

Couture: see *haute couture*.

Couturiers: the designers of *haute couture*.

Crêpe de chine: raw silk fabric with a crinkled texture.

Cropped: a short version of a garment; for example, a jacket ending at the waist.

Deadline: the latest time by which work may be delivered.

Designer label: well-made garments produced in small quantities.

Diffuser: a device for spraying liquid (such as fixative) evenly over an illustration.

Double-breasted: a garment with overlapping fronts, fastened with two rows of buttons.

Drape jacket: a long jacket of generous cut, with a single, low-buttoned fastening.

Epaulette: a decorative shoulder strap.

Fashion buyer: someone who selects and orders clothes from fashion houses for sale in shops and stores.

Fashion houses: established fashion design companies.

Flat colour: an even spread of colour, with no texture or detail.

Freelance: illustrator or designer who finds work with different companies.

Frock coat: a knee-length man's coat, with a flared skirt.

Graphic: vivid, life-like style of drawing or painting.

Haute couture (French for fine tailoring): a garment made for an individual customer.

Highlights: in drawing, light tone to emphasise prominent features.

House: *see* fashion house.

Laminate: to seal an illustration or photograph between two sheets of clear plastic.

Licence: an agreement whereby a large clothing manufacturer uses a designer's label for an agreed sum.

Life drawing: drawing human figures from live models.

Marbling: a mottled effect on paper, resembling marble.

Mass market: cheaply produced, ready-to-wear garments.

Mid-season: extra collection produced half-way through the spring/summer or autumn/winter collections.

Millinery: the design and making of hats.

Outer wear: garments worn outdoors, such as coats and jackets.

Overworking: in drawing, spoiling an illustration by adding too much detail.

Oxford bags: baggy trousers with wide bottoms.

Pattern: a diagram used as a guide for cutting out garments.

Pattern cutter: a skilled operator who draws out and sizes the working version of the pattern.

Portfolio: a large flat case in which illustrations are stored.

Ready-to-wear: garments produced in bulk for a wide range of customers.

Salon: a large room in *couture* houses, where exclusive fashion shows are presented.

Sample machinist: a skilled sewing machine operator who makes up the first version of a garment.

Tailoring: cutting, styling and hand-making a well-finished garment.

Template: a guide or pattern.

Toile: trial version of a garment, usually made in calico.

Trilby hat: a soft felt hat, with a dented crown and flexible brim.

Turn-up: a turned up fold at the bottom of a trouser leg.

PART TWO
MAKE-UP

Felicity Everett

Illustrated by Conny Jude

Consultant: Saskia Sarginson
Designed by Camilla Luff
Edited by Angela Wilkes

CONTENTS

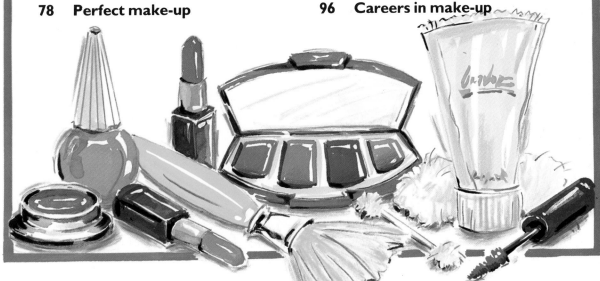

About this book

Make-up is exciting and colourful. You can wear as much, or as little, as you like. The important thing is to wear make-up which suits you and is right for the occasion.

This book shows you how to choose and put on make-up. It also gives you lots of ideas for ways to vary the basic looks in the book and invent some of your own.

Your make-up kit

Before you begin to experiment with make-up, you need to collect your make-up kit.

A few simple items go a long way. You can find out which basic things you need on pages 72-73.

Skincare

You can find out what kind of skin you have, and how to look after it on pages 68-69.

A daily cleansing routine

A really effective cleansing routine is important if you wear make-up. On pages 70-71, there is a

daily cleansing routine you can follow, and a table telling you which products suit your skin.

Choosing colours

Turn to page 74 for some hints on make-up shades to flatter your particular colouring.

Shaping and shading with colours

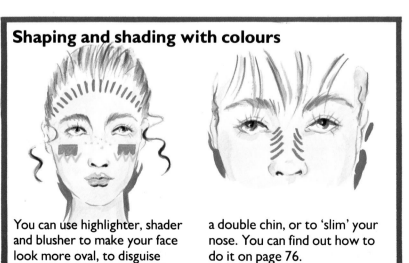

You can use highlighter, shader and blusher to make your face look more oval, to disguise

a double chin, or to 'slim' your nose. You can find out how to do it on page 76.

A perfect make-up

The make-up techniques in part two are illustrated step-by-step so you know exactly what to do.

Handy hints

Pictures in boxes this shape and size give tips on how to apply your make-up better.

The natural look

On page 82, you can find out how to do a natural-looking make-up, with the minimum of fuss.

Top-to-toe beauty treatment

The beauty routine on pages 84-85 includes conditioning treatment for your hair.

There are also recipes for home-made face masks using natural ingredients.

You can see how to give your hands a manicure and there are lots more ideas too.

Bright ideas for party make-up

From page 88 onwards, you will find some colourful and original ideas for party make-up.

The step-by-step instructions are as detailed as before, but the results are more dramatic.

Nostalgic looks

On pages 94-95, you can find out how to re-create nostalgic make-up looks from the past.

Looking after your skin

It is important to look after your skin properly, especially if you wear make-up.

To keep it healthy, you should cleanse and moisturise it each day. You will need:

Cleanser is cream or lotion which you use to clean your skin and take off your make-up. You can see how to do it on pages 70-71.

Moisturiser is cream or lotion which protects and softens your skin and stops it from becoming too dry. You can see how to put it on over the page.

Toner is liquid which closes up the pores after you have cleansed your skin and freshens it.

You can use a **cleansing bar** instead of cleanser, if your skin is oily. This looks like ordinary soap, but will not dry your skin.

Eye make-up remover can be liquid, or ready-to-use pads. It removes eye make-up gently.

Cotton buds are good for touching your face without making it greasy.

Cotton wool and tissues are useful for taking off your make-up and for putting on creams and lotions.

Diet

For clear healthy skin, eat plenty of fresh fruit and vegetables and drink lots of water. Don't eat sweets.

What skin type are you?

Look for skin care products which are recommended for your type of skin. If you don't know what type yours is, the simple test below will tell you whether your skin is dry, oily or normal. All you need is a roll of sticky tape.

Press a piece of sticky tape lightly over the bridge of your nose and on to your cheeks, avoiding the area round your eyes. Pull it off and look at it.

white flakes = dry skin
drops of moisture = oily skin
both = normal skin

Problem skin

If you often get rashes, look for hypo-allergenic products. They are made from pure ingredients which should not irritate your skin.

If you get lots of spots, use medicated skin products. *Never* squeeze spots. If you have a bad one, dab it gently with a cotton bud soaked in lemon juice.

KEY

DRY SKIN

Dry skin

Usually affects cheeks most – causes flaky patches, makes skin feel 'tight', after washing.

OILY SKIN

Oily skin

Often looks slightly shiny – usually affects nose, chin and forehead, sometimes tends to be spotty.

Normal skin

Dry in parts and oily in others – also called combination skin.

Cleansing

Follow this simple cleansing routine every morning* and evening.

1　Removing eye make-up

Apply make-up remover with cotton wool. Gently stroke it downwards and inwards towards the corner of each eye, making sure you do not pull the skin around your eyes.

2　Cleansing

If you use a cleansing bar, lather your face with a shaving brush, then rinse it off. Or you can smooth cream cleanser over your face and neck, then wipe it off gently with a tissue.

Finding the right products for your skin

This chart shows you which creams and lotions suit different types of skin.

To find out what type of skin you have, do the simple test on page 69.

Skin type	Cleanser	Toner	Moisturiser
Dry skin	Cream or thick liquid cleanser.	Mild toner: camomile, rose water, or still mineral water.	Cream moisturiser
Oily skin	Lotion or cleansing milk.	Natural astringent, such as witch hazel or cucumber.	Light, non-greasy liquid moisturiser.
Combination skin	Creamy liquid or cream cleanser.	Mild toner: camomile, rosewater or still mineral water.	Thin cream or thick lotion.

　　* You will not need to remove eye make-up in the morning.

3 Toning

Soak a cotton wool pad in toner and gently wipe it over your face. Or you can put the toner into an atomiser (an old, clean perfume spray would do) and spray it over your face.

4 Moisturising

Put little dots of moisturiser over your face and neck and gently rub it into your skin with your fingertips. You can put more on areas which are especially dry, such as your cheeks.

Deep cleansing

Deep cleansing about once a fortnight helps to keep your skin soft and really clean.

Any of the methods shown below work well. Used together, they make an excellent facial.

Facial sauna

Fill a big bowl with boiling water. Hold your face about 20cm from the water and drape a towel over your head to stop steam from escaping. Wait for five minutes.

Facial scrubs

Facial scrubs (or exfoliating creams) contain tiny granules which rub off the top layer of skin. Read the instructions on the packet for what to do.

Face masks*

You can buy gels, creams, or mud-based masks. Choose one which is recommended for your type of skin. Read the instructions on the packet for what to do.

* You will find some recipes for home-made face masks on page 85.

Your make-up kit

Here are the things you need to do a complete make-up, like the one on pages 78-81.

Face make-up

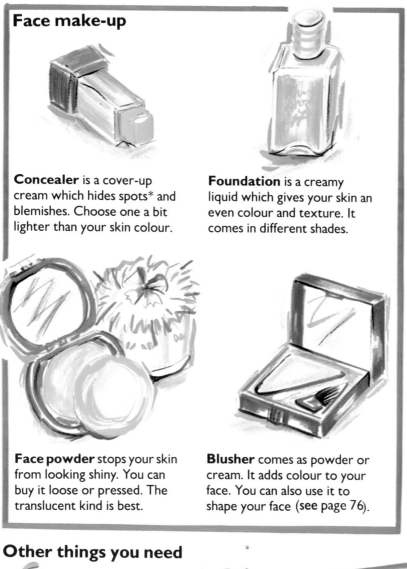

Concealer is a cover-up cream which hides spots* and blemishes. Choose one a bit lighter than your skin colour.

Foundation is a creamy liquid which gives your skin an even colour and texture. It comes in different shades.

Face powder stops your skin from looking shiny. You can buy it loose or pressed. The translucent kind is best.

Blusher comes as powder or cream. It adds colour to your face. You can also use it to shape your face (see page 76).

Lips

Lipstick adds colour and moisture to your lips. To put it on properly you need a lip pencil and a lip brush.

Lip gloss can be worn over lipstick, or on its own. It makes your lips look shiny and stops them from chapping.

Other things you need

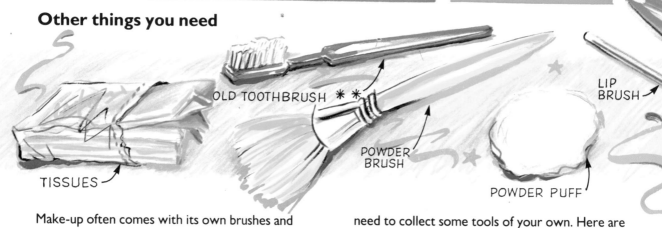

TISSUES

OLD TOOTHBRUSH **

POWDER BRUSH

POWDER PUFF

LIP BRUSH

Make-up often comes with its own brushes and applicators, but for a really professional look, you will need to collect some tools of your own. Here are some useful ones to start off with.

72   * You can buy medicated concealer especially for spots.   ** For combing your eyebrows.

Eye make-up

Eye-shadows come in different forms. To start with, choose two matching pressed powder eye-shadows.

You can also buy eye-shadow in pots (of powder or cream), in tubes (of cream), or in pencils (of powder or cream).

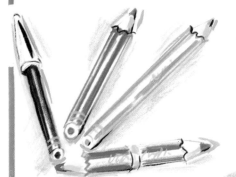

Eye pencil is for outlining your eyes, close to your eyelashes. Choose one a shade darker than your eye-shadow.

Mascara is thick liquid for darkening your eyelashes, you put it on with a brush. Use black or brown for everyday.

Professional make-up tips

Do not lend your make-up to anyone, even your best friend. You can pass on eye infections and cold sores.

To check that your foundation is the right colour for you, test it on your face (without any make-up on).

Keep your pencils sharp. You can sharpen them better if you put them in the fridge for an hour before you need them.

Keep your make-up in a clean, dry place. A box with compartments, such as a plastic tool box is ideal.

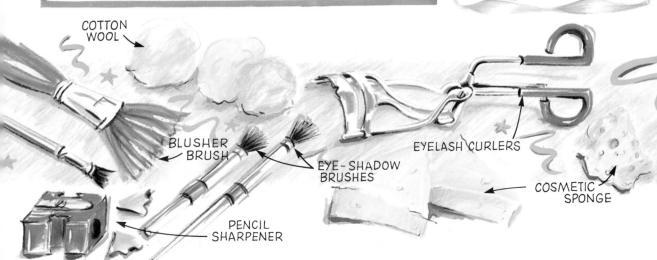

COTTON WOOL

BLUSHER BRUSH

EYE-SHADOW BRUSHES

EYELASH CURLERS

COSMETIC SPONGE

PENCIL SHARPENER

Choosing colours

It is fun trying out make-up colours, but mistakes can be expensive. It is best to choose shades which go with your colouring.

Here are six typical hair and skin colours. Below each picture, you can see the make-up colours which flatter that type.

Fair skin/brown hair

Brunettes often have fair skin and rosy cheeks. If your skin looks blotchy, even it out with a creamy-beige foundation.

Fair skin/blonde hair

Blondes have fair, rather dry skin which needs careful skin care. Use a pinkish foundation to give colour to your skin.

Freckled skin/red hair

Redheads tend to have fair, sensitive, freckled skin. Choose a light foundation which lets your freckles show through.

Blusher

TAWNY PINK

GOLDEN PEACH

Blusher

BEIGE PINK

PEACH

Blusher

AMBER

DUSKY PINK

Eyes

GRASS GREEN
SAND BROWN
APRICOT
GOLD
BLUE

Eyes

CORNFLOWER BLUE
PINKY MAUVE
SOFT BROWN
VIOLET
GREY

Eyes

GOLDEN BROWN
SAGE GREEN
TAWNY PINK
PLUM
RUST

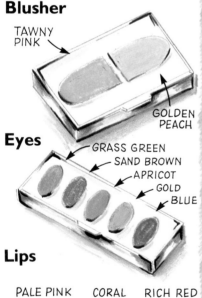

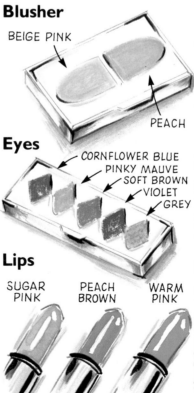

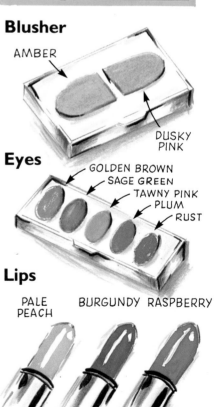

Lips

PALE PINK   CORAL   RICH RED

Lips

SUGAR PINK   PEACH BROWN   WARM PINK

Lips

PALE PEACH   BURGUNDY   RASPBERRY

Several companies make foundations and concealers especially for dark skin. You can mix two colours together if you cannot find the right shade.

Do not wear powder. It will just make your skin look dull. Let it s natural sheen show through a light coating of foundation.

Black skin/dark hair

Black skin can be oily and sometimes the colour is a little uneven. Even it out with a light, non-greasy foundation.

Brown skin/dark hair

Brown skin can be slightly blotchy. Mix foundation and concealer and then use the mixture to even out your colouring.

Olive skin/dark hair

Olive skin can look sallow and may be oily, but a non-greasy, dark beige foundation can make it look healthy and golden.

Blusher

BRICK RED

BURGUNDY

Eyes

GOLDEN BROWN
BUTTERCUP
NAVY BLUE
ORANGE
ROSE

Lips

WINE RED   PILLAR-BOX RED   SHOCKING PINK

Blusher

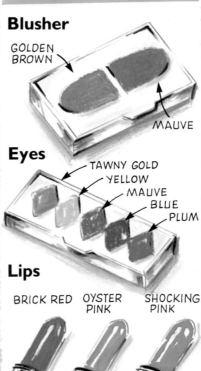

GOLDEN BROWN

MAUVE

Eyes

TAWNY GOLD
YELLOW
MAUVE
BLUE
PLUM

Lips

BRICK RED   OYSTER PINK   SHOCKING PINK

Blusher

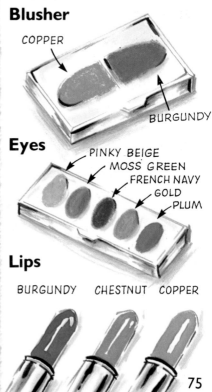

COPPER

BURGUNDY

Eyes

PINKY BEIGE
MOSS GREEN
FRENCH NAVY
GOLD
PLUM

Lips

BURGUNDY   CHESTNUT   COPPER

75

Shaping and shading

Here you can find out how to use shader, highlighter and blusher to make your face look more oval, and show off your best features.

The right hairstyle can also help to enhance the shape of your face. Turn to pages 138-139 to see how.

The key below shows you exactly where to put your highlighter, shader and blusher. Blend them in well, so no hard edges show.

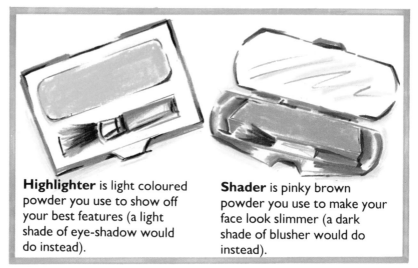

Highlighter is light coloured powder you use to show off your best features (a light shade of eye-shadow would do instead).

Shader is pinky brown powder you use to make your face look slimmer (a dark shade of blusher would do instead).

What shape is your face?

LONG FACE

ROUND FACE

HEART-SHAPED FACE

SQUARE FACE

KEY

SHADER   /////

HIGHLIGHTER WWW

BLUSHER   ▬

Pull your hair back from your face and look at it in the mirror. Compare your face shape with the four basic shapes shown here. Then look at the key to find out where to put your highlighter, shader and blusher.

76

Shader

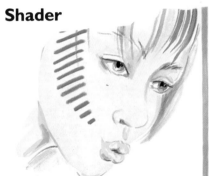

To make your cheekbones look higher, suck in your cheeks and dot shader in the hollows below them. Blend it in from your cheeks towards your hairline.

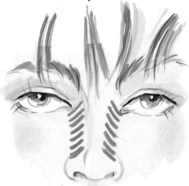

To make your nose look slimmer, dot a little shader down each side of it, or wherever your nose is uneven. Blend it in evenly with the tip of your finger.

To disguise a double chin, dab a little shader just beneath your chin and blend it in well around your jawline. Make sure it does not look like a dirty tide mark.

Highlighter

To highlight high cheekbones, dot a little highlighter just above your cheekbones and blend it in evenly, so it slants upwards towards your hairline.

If you have attractive eyes, dab a little highlighter on to each browbone (the area just beneath your eyebrows). Blend it in so that it barely shows.

If your mouth is your best feature, use a lip brush to stroke a little highlighter into the dimple above your top lip. Blend it in evenly so it barely shows.

Blusher

You can use blusher to give your face a better shape, as well as to give it colour. Blend it in to your highlighter and shader so that no hard lines show.

To give a hint of colour to your whole face, dot a little blusher on to each earlobe, as shown. Then blend it in well with your brush, so it barely shows.

If you are looking pale, dab a little blusher around your hairline, as shown. Then blend it in thoroughly so there is just a hint of colour showing.

Step-by-step to a perfect make-up

Getting ready

Put your make-up on in a room with a large mirror and lots of light. You can find out what make-up you need on pages 72-73.

Tie your hair out of the way, or put on a headband. Wash your face and put on moisturiser. Now you are ready to begin.

Concealer

Dot a little concealer over any spots, blemishes or dark shadows and blend it in well with the tip of your finger.

Foundation

Dot a little foundation over your face. Put it over your lips too, but not your eyelids, as it will make them oily.

Wet your cosmetic sponge in warm water, then squeeze most of the water out and blot it on a piece of tissue.

Use the sponge to spread the foundation evenly over your face. Make sure you smooth it in well under your chin.

Powder

Dip a ball of cotton wool into your tub of loose powder, then pat it firmly, but gently all over your face until it is evenly covered.

Use a large, soft powder brush to flick off the spare powder. Brush it downwards to make the tiny hairs on your face lie flat.

If a stubborn spot still shows through foundation and powder, dab a clean brush on your concealer and paint it out.

Blusher

Stroke your blusher brush across your palette of powder blusher until it is lightly, but evenly, coated with powder.

Brush the blusher on to your cheekbones (this is the area just above your cheeks), and right up to your hairline.

Keep adding more until the colour is strong enough. If it starts to look too obvious, you can tone it down with powder.

Professional make-up tips

To find out what colour blusher you need, lightly pinch the skin on your cheeks. The colour which appears is the shade of blusher you need.

Do not put your make-up on straight after a bath or shower as your skin is more flushed than usual. Wait until it cools down and returns to normal.

You can re-cycle old lipstick ends by heating them in a bowl over a pan of boiling water. Put the mixture in a pot to go solid. Put it on with a brush.

To make your eyelashes look extra thick, dust them with face powder then brush away the excess, before you put on your mascara.

Check your finished face make-up to make sure there are no hard lines of colour anywhere.

If you can see any, blend them in with a brush. Now you are ready to make up your eyes and lips.

Eyes

Eye-shadow

SPONGE TIP

Brushing eyebrows

Start by stroking the lighter shade of eye-shadow over your eyelids, as shown. Blend it in with an eye-shadow brush.

Stroke the darker shade of eye-shadow on to the outer half of your eyelids, as shown. Blend in the edges with another brush.

Brush your eyebrows upwards with an old toothbrush. Then smooth them in the direction they grow, with your fingertip.

Eye pencil

Draw a fine pencil line along your eyelids, next to your lashes, as shown. Smudge the line slightly with a damp cotton bud.

Draw another line underneath your eyes, close to your lower lashes, as shown, and smudge it gently, as before.

If you want to put pencil on the inner rim of your eye, use one which is not too sharp and draw it on carefully.

Curling eyelashes

Mascara

Clamp the eyelash curlers round your top lashes very carefully. Hold them shut for a minute, then open them again.

Look into a hand mirror, held at chin level. Brush mascara on to your top lashes. Let it dry, then put on a second coat.

Look straight ahead into your make-up mirror to put mascara on your bottom lashes. You only need to put on one coat.

80

Lips

Outlining your lips

Draw an outline around the edge of your mouth with a lip pencil, resting your little finger on your chin to steady your hand.

You can use a fine lip brush to outline your mouth, if you want. Dab it on your lipstick, then paint in the outline.

Putting on lipstick

Coat your lip brush with colour from your lipstick. Carefully paint the colour on to your lips, keeping within the outline.

Blotting your lipstick

Blot your lipstick on a tissue (taking care not to smudge it). Then put on a second coat and blot your lips again.

Lip gloss

To give your lips some shine, dot lip gloss in the centre of your lips and carefully brush it outwards towards the edges.

This make-up is good for evenings, when you want to make a special effort to look good.

Allow plenty of time to do it. You can see how to do a quick, simple make-up over the page.

The natural look

All you need for a simple, natural looking make-up are the things shown here.

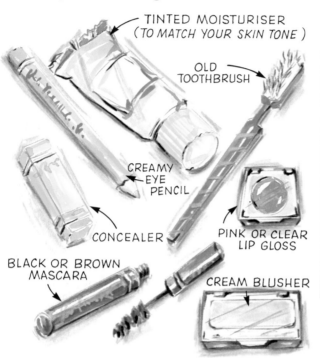

TINTED MOISTURISER
(TO MATCH YOUR SKIN TONE)

OLD TOOTHBRUSH

CREAMY EYE PENCIL

CONCEALER

PINK OR CLEAR LIP GLOSS

BLACK OR BROWN MASCARA

CREAM BLUSHER

1 Concealer and tinted moisturiser

Tie your hair back. Wash your face and pat it dry. Cover any blemishes with concealer (see page 78). Dot moisturiser on with your finger and smooth it in.

2 Blusher

Use your fingertips to dot blusher on to your cheeks, then carefully smooth the blusher outwards and upwards towards your hairline.

3 Eye pencil

Carefully draw a pencil line across your eyelid, next to your eyelashes. Then smooth the colour over your eyelid, using a damp cotton bud, or your fingertip.

82   *This make-up goes well with the natural jewellery on pages 106-109 and the pretty jewellery on pages 111-116.

4 Mascara

Brush mascara on to your upper lashes, as on page 80. Let it dry and then apply a second coat. Brush one coat of mascara on to your lower lashes.

5 Brushing your eyebrows

Use an old toothbrush to brush your eyebrows upwards. Then wet your finger and smooth it over each eyebrow in the direction it grows.

6 Lip gloss

Using a lip brush, paint lip gloss carefully on to your lips. Do not brush it right to the edge of your mouth, as it can 'run' and look rather messy.

7 The finished look

This is what the finished make-up should look like. With a bit of practise, you will be able to do it in a matter of minutes.

Top-to-toe beauty routine

It you are planning a special night out and want to look and feel your best, give yourself an all-over beauty treatment, following this step-by-step plan.

Set aside a few hours (you will need at least two) so that you can relax and really enjoy yourself. If you are going out with a friend, you could ask her over so you can have fun getting ready together.

Having a bath

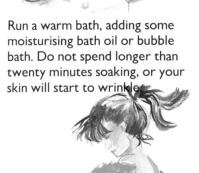

Run a warm bath, adding some moisturising bath oil or bubble bath. Do not spend longer than twenty minutes soaking, or your skin will start to wrinkle.

While you are in the bath, take a handful of coarse sea salt and rub it over your bottom and thighs to stimulate your circulation and make you tingle.

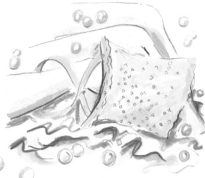

Then massage your skin all over with a textured bath mitt. Its rough surface will rub off any dead skin and leave your body feeling soft and smooth.

Get out of the bath and pat yourself dry with a soft towel. Dust some talc over your feet and under your arms (use deodorant under your arms, if you prefer).

Massage a moisturising body lotion all over your body (if your skin is dry, use body oil). Pay special attention to dry skin on your heels and elbows.

Conditioning your hair

Warm two tablespoons of olive oil or almond oil in a saucepan (do not let it get too hot, or it will scald you). Massage it into your hair until it is all absorbed.

Wrap a piece of clingfilm around your hair, overlapping it at the front. Scrunch it up to seal the ends together. Make sure you do not drip oil on your clothes.

Then wrap a warm towel round your head in a turban. Leave it on for thirty minutes. You can see how to wash out the oil over the page.

Putting on a face mask

While your hair conditioner is working, put on a face mask (see below for recipes). You can find out how to do this on page 71.

You can put thin slices of cucumber or potato on your eyes if you like. This soothes them.

Put on some soothing music, lie back and relax for ten minutes. Then rinse off the face mask with warm water and pat your face dry with a soft towel.

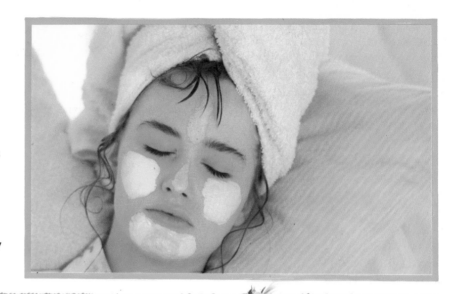

Home-made face masks

For dry skin: mix together a tablespoon of plain yogurt, a teaspoon of runny honey and a mashed, ripe avocado. Spread the mixture on your face and leave it on for ten to fifteen minutes.

For oily skin: mix together a tablespoon of plain yogurt, a teaspoon of honey, a teaspoon of oatmeal and a mashed peach. Spread it on your face and leave for ten minutes.

For normal skin: crush a few thick slices of cucumber to a pulp and mix them with a teaspoon of plain yogurt and a few drops of rose water. Spread the mixture on your face and leave it on for fifteen minutes.

Removing unwanted hair

Everyone has hair on their legs, but there is no need to remove it unless you really want to.

Depilatory cream is the gentlest and easiest method of removing hair. It is safer than shaving and less painful than waxing your legs.

If you decide to remove the hair on your legs, it is best to remove it regularly. The hairs that grow back look thicker, because they are short and stubbly.

Read the instructions on the packet before you start. Squeeze some cream into the palm of your hand, then spread it thickly over your legs with your fingers.

Leave it on for as long as the packet tells you to. Then wipe it off gently with a wet cloth. Rinse your legs and then pat them dry with a towel.

Washing your hair

When your conditioning hair oil has been on for half an hour, wash it off. Shampoo your hair twice and rinse it thoroughly to remove every trace of the oil.

Comb your hair very gently to remove any tangles. Start at the ends of your hair and work back towards your head. Do not tug the comb through clumps of your hair.

If you are blow drying your hair, do it in sections. Hold the hair dryer at least 10cm from your hair and keep it moving, as you dry, to avoid damaging your hair.

Styling your hair

You can buy soft, fabric hair curlers like the ones in the photograph which will curl your hair without damaging it. You can make corkscrew curls or soft waves.

Put them in your hair and leave them for 45 minutes. Meanwhile you can give yourself a manicure and pedicure (see below and opposite).

When you take the curlers out, gently brush your hair, or just run your fingers through it, to separate the curls.

Your hands

Treat your hands to a manicure before you go out. First, file your nails with an emery board. It is best to file from the edges to the centre of your nails.

Then soak your fingertips in warm, soapy water for a few minutes. If your nails are dirty, scrub them with a nailbrush. Dry your hands. Then rub on some hand cream.

Rub some cuticle cream into the hard pads of skin at the base of your nails to soften them. Then gently push back the cuticle with a cotton bud.

Carefully paint on a thin coat of nail varnish. There are some ideas for party nails on page 89. When the varnish is dry, carefully put on another coat.

Your feet

Now you can give yourself a pedicure. Trim your toenails straight across with nail clippers. Then file them from the edges inwards.

Soften your cuticles with cream and push them back. Then separate your toes with cotton wool* and put on two coats of varnish.

Plucking your eyebrows

Before you put your make-up on, tidy your eyebrows by plucking any straggly hairs that grow beneath them. Pluck them in the direction they grow.

Make-up

Now you can put on your make-up. First, tie your hair back and put some moisturiser on your face. Then turn to pages 88-95 for some ideas on party make-up.

Scent

If you wear scent, such as toilet water or perfume, dab a little on your pulse points (behind your ears and knees and on the inside of your wrists and elbows).

Ready to go

Now you can get dressed. Make sure you don't spoil your hair or smudge your make-up. Check your appearance in a full length mirror before you go out.

* You can buy foam toe pads from the chemists, which do the same thing.

Party make-up

Party make-up can be anything from bold eyeshadow and bright lipstick, to false eyelashes, sequins and turquoise mascara. Here are some things to collect.

CHILDREN'S FACE PAINTS

STAGE MAKE-UP *

NAIL VARNISH IN UNUSUAL COLOURS

FALSE EYELASHES

SEQUINS AND STARS

Eye-shadows

You can buy little pots of loose, sparkly powder eye-shadow in lots of colours. To stop it from spilling on to your cheeks, put it on with a damp brush.

Mascara

You can buy mascara in lots of bright colours, such as violet and green. If you want a hint of colour, brush it on to the tips of your lashes only.

Eyebrows

You can colour your eyebrows to match your mascara. Dab a little mascara on your eyebrow brush. Blot the brush on a tissue, then brush your eyebrows with it.

False eye-lashes

Put these on before your eye-shadow. Apply a coat of mascara, then dot eyelash glue along the lash band with a pin. Make sure you glue each end.

Let the glue dry for a second. Then pick up the lashes with a pair of tweezers and position them on your closed eyelid, on top of your real lashes.

Gently press the lash band down on to your eyelid with your finger. Wait for the glue to dry, then brush the eyelashes upwards with an old toothbrush.

88   * If you have difficulty finding stage make-up, you can write to Charles Fox Ltd, theatre make-up suppliers, 22 Tavistock St, London WC2.

SHIMMERY POWDER EYE-SHADOW

COLOURED MASCARA

GLITTER DUST

TEMPORARY HAIR COLOUR

FROSTED BLUSHER

Designer finger nails

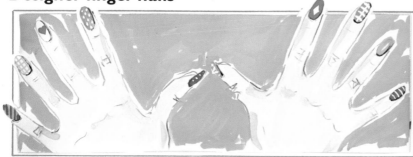

Manicure your nails as on page 86. Then put on nail varnish. You can buy it in lots of bright colours. Use two or more colours to paint on spots, stripes, checks or any design you like. If you are using more than one colour, make sure each coat is thoroughly dry before you apply the next, or your nail varnish will smudge.

Glitter dust and sequins

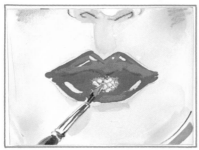

You can make shimmery lip gloss by mixing some glitter dust with your ordinary lip gloss in the palm of your hand. Then brush it on your lips, in the usual way.

Add shine to your make-up by glueing sequins on your face with eyelash glue. Put them at the outer corners of your eyes, or glue one on as a beauty spot.

Colouring your hair

You can change your hair colour for the evening, using a wash in/wash out hair colour mousse or shampoo, in an unusual colour.

Another way of adding flashes of colour to your hair, is to attach thin swatches of false hair to your own, using slides or ribbons.

Polka dot make-up

This party make-up combines the sophistication of black and white with the fun of polka dots for a stunning effect.

You will need

light beige foundation
translucent powder
white and dark grey powder eye-
  shadows
black eye pencil
black mascara
pale pink or white lipstick
matching lip pencil

Foundation

First, smooth foundation all over your face and neck, using a cosmetic sponge. You can check the techniques for applying this make-up on page 78-81.

Powder

Then powder your face quite thickly using a cotton wool ball, or a powder puff and gently flick off any spare powder with your powder brush.

Eye-shadow

Brush a thick layer of white eye-shadow over the whole of your eyelid, as shown. You may need two coats to get the heavy, matt effect shown here.

Sharpen your eye pencil until you get a really good point. Then, warm the tip of your pencil in the palm of your hand, so it goes on thickly.

Then brush dark grey eye-shadow along the line of your eye socket as shown, broadening the line towards the outer corner of your eye. Blend it in with a brush.

Draw pencil dots on your eyelids, as shown. Press firmly but gently with the tip of the pencil, turning it slightly at the same time, so the dots show up well.

Eye pencil

Carefully draw a fine black pencil line along your eyelid, close to your upper eyelashes. Then smudge it slightly with a damp cotton bud, or your finger.

Mascara

Curl your eyelashes with eyelash curlers, then brush mascara on to your upper lashes. Let it dry, then put on a second coat. Put one coat on your lower lashes.

Brushing eyebrows

Brush your eyebrows with your eyebrow brush. Then dip the tip of your finger in a little Vaseline and smooth it over your eyebrows to make them shine.

Lipstick

Outline your lips with a fine brush, or a lip pencil which matches your lipstick. Then put on your lipstick. Blot it on a tissue, apply another coat and blot again.

Too pale?

If you think your finished make-up looks too pale, brush on a little pink blusher. Make sure you blend it in well.

Hair

If you have short hair, smooth it back with hair gel. If your hair is long, tie it back, then tie a scarf round your head in a big, floppy bow, as shown.

If you have a fringe, put setting lotion* on it, then use curling tongs** to make it wavy. Comb it upwards and spray hairspray on it to make it stand up.

Wear black and white clothes with this look, for maximum effect.

There is another quite different party make-up on the next page.

* You can find out more about setting lotion on page 173.
** You can see how to use curling tongs on page 174.

Razzle dazzle make-up

You are sure to be noticed in this colourful party make-up. You can use different colours from the ones shown here if you like.

You will need

foundation
translucent powder
golden peach blusher
orange, sea green and smoky
  grey eye-shadows
black and emerald green mascara
orange lipstick
matching lip pencil and lip brush
gold lip gloss

Foundation

First, smooth foundation all over your face and neck, using a cosmetic sponge. You can check the techniques for putting on make-up on pages 78-81.

Powder

Then powder your face lightly all over, using a cotton wool ball or a powder puff. Gently flick off any loose powder with your powder brush.

Blusher

Brush blusher on to your cheeks, as shown. You can put on a little more in the evening than you would during the day, but make sure you blend it in well.

Eye-shadow

Brush orange eye-shadow on to the inner half of one eyelid and the outer half of the other eyelid. You can put on quite a lot, as long as you blend it in well.

Brush green eye-shadow on to the other half of each eyelid and blend it in well where it meets the orange eyeshadow, so that the two colours merge.

Dampen a fine tipped brush and use it to stroke grey eye-shadow in a fine line along your upper lash line and at the outer corners of the lower lashes.

Mascara

Brush black mascara on to your upper and lower eye lashes (you can see how on page 80). When it is dry, brush a second coat on your upper lashes.

Brush emerald green mascara carefully on to the tips of your eyelashes. If you want a stronger shade of green, wait for it to dry, then put on a second coat.

Brushing eyebrows

Brush your eyebrows upwards (you can put a little brown eye-shadow on the brush if you want to darken them). Then smooth them with your finger.

Lipstick

Outline your lips with your orange lip pencil (or a lip brush coated with lipstick). Fill in the colour with your orange lipstick and a lip brush keeping within the outline.

Lip gloss

Brush a little gold lip gloss on to the middle of your lower lip to make your lips look fuller. You could use non-toxic gold eye-shadow instead.

Hair

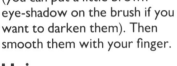

If you have long hair which is not naturally curly, curl it as on pages 165-166. Then tie a brightly coloured scarf round your head in a big, floppy bow.

If you have a fringe, pull a few wispy strands of it down in front of your eyes and then gently finger a little hair gel* through it to separate the curls.

This razzle dazzle make-up looks especially good worn with the bright jewellery on pages 100-105 of part three.

* You can find out more about hair gel on page 173.

Four nostalgic looks

Here you can find out how to create some distinctive make-up looks from the twenties, forties, fifties and sixties.

On pages 148-149 there are some more ideas for nostalgic hair styles which would go well with these looks.

The 1920s

In the 1920s girls wore bold eye make-up, bright lipstick and sometimes a false beauty spot. They often had their hair bobbed.

You will need: pale foundation, translucent powder, dark eye-shadow, black mascara, dark eyebrow pencil, glossy pink or red lipstick and a matching lip pencil or lip brush.

Face: put on your foundation and powder.

Eyes: brush eye-shadow over your eyelids and browbones. Smudge a little under your lower lashes. Then put on lots of mascara. Pencil in narrow, arched eyebrows.

Lips: were painted in a very distinctive shape in the twenties. Outline them with lip pencil to emphasize your 'Cupid's Bow' (the dimple in your top lip). Then put on your lipstick, being careful to keep within the outline.

Finally, paint or stick on a false beauty spot, as shown.

The 1940s

Make-up was bold and glamorous in the 1940s. Girls painted on dark eyebrows and bright red lips. They often wore their hair elegantly rolled at the front, and left the back loose round their shoulders.

You will need: pale foundation, translucent powder, dark blusher (in brown or plum), grey or brown eye pencil, eyebrow pencil, glossy red lipstick and matching lip pencil, or a lip brush.

Face: put on your foundation and powder. Brush blusher high on your cheekbones.

Eyes: brush eye-shadow on your eyelids, close to your eyelashes. Put mascara on your top lashes only. Thicken and darken your eyebrows with eyebrow pencil.

Lips: outline them carefully with your lip pencil, squaring off the bottom lip slightly, as shown. Then paint them with two or three coats of lipstick, keeping within the outline. Blot your lips between each coat, so your lipstick will stay on longer.

The 1950s

Fifties make-up concentrated on the eyes. Black eyeliner swept up at the corners gave eyes a cat-like look. Girls wore their hair in high pony tails, with the front rolled, or worn in a short, neat fringe.

You will need: light beige foundation, slightly lighter powder, pink blusher, light blue or yellow eye-shadow, liquid eyeliner, a few false eyelashes, eyelash glue, mascara, pink lip pencil and pale pink pearly lipstick.

Face: put on your foundation, powder and blusher.

Eyes: brush eye-shadow on to your eyelids. Carefully paint a narrow line of liquid eyeliner close to your top eyelashes, winging it upwards slightly at the outer corners of your eyes.

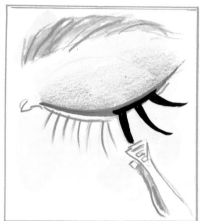

Cut small sections off complete false eyelashes and stick them at the outer corners of your eyes with eyelash glue, as shown. Brush two coats of mascara on to your upper lashes only.

Lips: outline them with lip pencil and fill in with lipstick.

The 1960s

Girls in the 1960s wore a lot of dark eye make-up. Faces and lips were as pale as possible. Girls wore their hair in short, boyish haircuts, or backcombed into a glamorous 'bouffant' style.

You will need: pale foundation and powder, pale matt eye-shadow (pink or white), grey eye pencil, black liquid eyeliner, false eyelashes, eyelash glue, black eye pencil, black mascara, pale matt lipstick.

Face: put on your foundation and powder.

Eyes: brush on your eye-shadow. Draw a thickish line of grey eye pencil along the rim of your socket and smudge it slightly. Then, paint a line of liquid eyeliner along your top eyelashes.

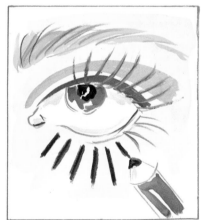

Glue false eyelashes on to your upper eyelids (see page 88 for the method). Then draw in false eyelashes underneath your eyes with black eye pencil. Put on several coats of mascara.

Lips: cover them with foundation, then put on your lipstick.

Careers in make-up

There is a wide variety of career opportunities in the make-up industry.

Below you can find out about some of the more popular occupations.

In-store beauty consultant

Description: working for a large cosmetic firm, promoting and selling their goods within a department store. They advise customers on which products would suit their skin and colouring, and occasionally do a make-up or demonstration session.

Qualifications: most cosmetic firms give intensive in-house training. They prefer you to have some experience in retailing (preferably cosmetics) first, although personality counts for a lot.

Personal qualities: a large proportion of your time is spent talking to customers, encouraging them to buy your company's products, so you must have an outgoing personality which inspires confidence in people. You will also spend much of your time on your feet, so need to be physically fit.

Getting started: get some retail experience by working in a shop or department store, then apply to the major cosmetic companies. Alternatively, go to work for a department store which sells own-brand make-up, as they often recruit beauty consultants from their own staff.

Beauty therapist

Description: providing a very wide range of both facial and body treatments, from skin cleansing and care to infra-red and ultra-violet treatment, giving advice on nutrition and so on. Beauty therapists' often work in consultation with the client's doctor.

Qualifications: there are a wide range of courses available, most of which have quite high academic requirements for entry.

Personal qualities: as with a beautician, you must have confidence, dexterity, and the ability to get on well with people. You must also look well-groomed, and be prepared to work unsocial hours (most people will only be available to see you after working hours).

Getting started: apply for a place on a full-time course as a beauty therapist, or one which combines hairdressing and beauty therapy. Private and evening courses are also available, however, you should always check that the course is recognised by your local education authority before enrolling.

Beautician or beauty specialist

Description: giving clients facial treatments such as make-up, eyelash dyeing and eyebrow plucking. Can also involve techniques such as hair removal, manicures and pedicures.

Qualifications: apprenticeship and/or formal qualifications. Most courses are fee-paying.

Personal qualities: you should always look well-groomed in order to gain the client's trust. The ability to get on well with people, and put clients at ease is essential. You also need confidence and a steady hand.

Getting started: enrol on a course, or approach salons or specialist clinics to see whether they have apprenticeships.

Make-up for theatre

Description: advising on the whole area of make-up, hair, wigs, costumes and special effects. Sometimes, but not always, doing actors' make up.

Qualifications: courses are available in theatre studies. These normally include an introduction to theatre make-up. A period of apprenticeship with a large wig-making firm would be an added bonus.

Personal qualities: imagination, artistic flair and love of the theatre. You also need diplomacy and tact, as you will be dealing with actors as they are about to go on stage and may be on edge.

Getting there: enrol at a reputable college. Gain as much experience within the theatre as possible. Apply to large theatre companies.

PART THREE
JEWELRY

Felicity Everett and Carol Garbera

Illustrated by Lily Whitlock
and Chris Lyon
Edited by Janet Cook
Designed by Camilla Luff

Contents

About jewelry

The jewelry in part three is stylish, simple and cheap to make. This part is divided into five sections, each showing a different style of jewelry. You might want to make all the things in one section, or choose a few items from each. Since there is something to suit most tastes, you can make jewelry as presents, or even to sell. You can see the five styles below.

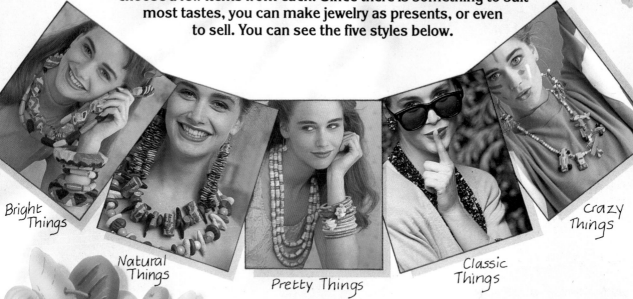

Bright Things

Natural Things

Pretty Things

Classic Things

Crazy Things

Things you need

Clay

Pliers

Yarn

You can see what materials, tools and equipment you need to make the jewelry on pages 126-127 (you may already have some of them). Try to work tidily – it is easy to spoil a piece of jewelry while working on a messy surface.

Instructions

Clear instructions, illustrated step-by-step, explain how to make each item. All the basic skills, such as making papier mâché or clay beads, are clearly labelled, so you can refer back to them if you get stuck.

Design hints

The book shows certain colors and designs for each piece of jewelry, but you can choose your own. Design hints, in colored boxes like this, suggest simple ways of adapting the jewelry.

Choosing what to make

Each section has a patterned border at the top of every page so you can easily see where it starts and ends. Every item of jewelry is coded so you can tell how long it takes and what it costs to make (see the key opposite).

Key

▲	up to 2 hours	●	very cheap
▲ ▲	up to 1 day	● ●	cheap
▲ ▲ ▲	1 to 2 days	● ● ●	quite cheap
▲ ▲ ▲ ▲	2 days or more	● ● ● ●	more expensive

Bright things

In this section you will find bold jewelry, painted in bright, abstract patterns. Most of it is made from papier mâché, which takes a few days to dry. But if you are patient, you will be rewarded with stunning results. Below are some of the things you can make.

Papier mâché bangle

Paper earrings

Papier mâché brooch

Papier mâché necklace

Paper necklace

This jewelry looks especially striking if you wear it with **Razzle dazzle** make-up. See page 92 to find out how to put it on.

Making papier mâché

The quantities listed below are for the earrings, necklace, brooch and bangle. Make less if you only want to make one or two items.

For the paste: 1¼ liters (about 2¼ pints) warm water to 250g (8-10oz) plain white flour. In addition you need two or three old newspapers, a dishpan and a spoon.

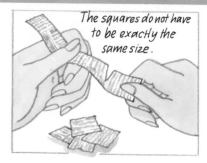

The squares do not have to be exactly the same size.

Tear the newspaper into 2cm (¾in) squares. To make the paste, gradually mix water into the flour in the pan, until there are no lumps.

Then stir in the newspaper and leave it to stand for two or three hours, until the paper goes really soft. The papier mâché is then ready to use.

Papier mâché necklace ▲▲▲▲ ●●

You will need:
½ ltr (about ¾ pt) papier mâché
poster paints, fine paint brush and jar
paper varnish and varnish brush
3 or 4 4mm* knitting needles OR
16 to 20 toothpicks
Vaseline
about 1¼ m (1¼ yd) metallic cord and a darning needle
old potato
sandpaper
transparent tape

If you want to make chunky beads, cover the knitting needles with a thin coat of Vaseline. For finer beads, do the same with toothpicks.

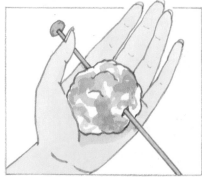

Take enough papier mâché in your hand to make the size of bead you want. Press the knitting needle or toothpick into it, as shown.

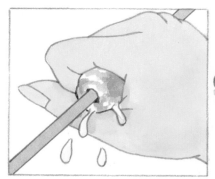

Then mold the papier mâché around the knitting needle, squeezing out the spare paste. Smooth it with your fingers until it is the shape you want.

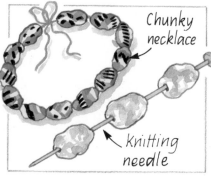

Chunky necklace

Knitting needle

To make a chunky necklace, you will need to make 12 papier mâché beads 5cm (2in) long. You should be able to fit three on each knitting needle.

Fine necklace

Toothpicks

To make a finer necklace, make 16-20 beads 4cm (1½in) long. Make each one on a toothpick. You can see how to paint them over the page.

*English size 8, or US size 5.

Bright things 2

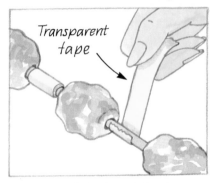

Necklace (continued)

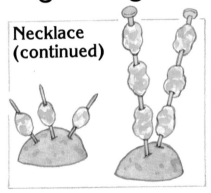

Cut a potato in half and stick the knitting needles or toothpicks into it, as shown. Leave the beads to dry* like this for three to five days.

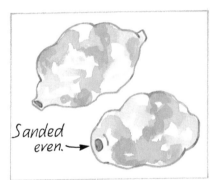

Sanded even.

When the outsides are dry, slide the beads off the needles and leave them for a day, so that the middles dry. Then sandpaper the ends to improve the shape.

Transparent tape

Now thread the beads back on to the needles or picks and wind transparent tape around the needle in between each one, to keep them separate.

Below are some ideas for patterns and color combinations.

Painting your beads

POSTER PAINT

Paint two coats of white poster paint on each bead. This evens out the surface, making it easier to paint your pattern on later. Leave them to dry.

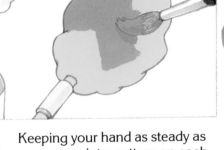

Keeping your hand as steady as you can, paint a pattern on each bead. Begin with the lightest color you want to use and let one dry before using another.

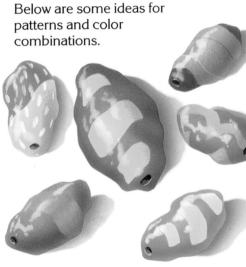

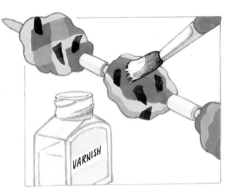

VARNISH

When the paint is dry, keep the beads on the needles, and brush on a thin coat of paper varnish. Let it dry, then brush on a second coat.

Darning needle

When the varnish is dry, slide the beads off the needles and thread them on to your metallic cord with a darning needle. Tie the ends in a secure bow.

Design hint

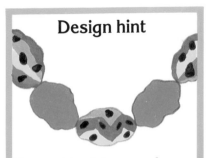

You could paint some of your beads with a plain color that matches the patterned ones. Then make a necklace by threading up alternate plain and patterned beads.

*The beads will dry more quickly in summer than in winter. Do not try to dry them over direct heat.

Papier mâché bangle ▲▲▲▲ ●

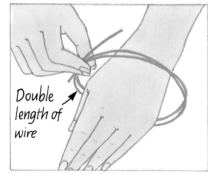

Double length of wire →

Cut** a length of wire long enough to fit twice around the widest part of your hand with a bit to spare. Twist it into a circle to make your bangle base.

Cover an old plate with a thin layer of Vaseline. Using this as your work surface, mold handfuls of papier mâché roughly around the wire base.

When you have covered all the wire, mold the papier mâché into a smooth, even shape. Leave it in a warm place for several days until it feels dry.

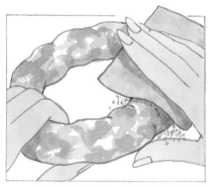

Sandpaper the edges smooth. Then paint it as for the beads (you do not need to paint a pattern on the inside). When dry, brush on two coats of varnish.

Two finished bangles.

Papier mâché brooch ▲▲▲▲ ●

Working on a greased plate, shape the papier mâché into a disc with a flat base, about 6cm (2½in) in diameter and 1cm (½in) thick. Leave it to dry.

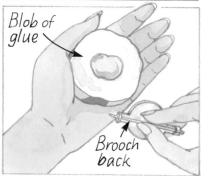

Blob of glue →

Brooch back →

Then paint it as for the beads. Paint the back a plain color. Varnish it when the paint is dry. When the varnish is dry, glue a brooch pin on the back.

*You can buy fuse wire from a hardware store.   **Use wire cutters or old scissors to cut it with.

Bright things 3

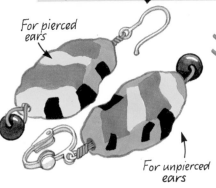

Papier mâché earrings ▲▲▲ ●

You will need:

2 big papier mâché beads (see page 5)
1 pair clips (with loops for dangly earrings) or ball hooks
40cm (about 16in) of 0·6mm (⅛in) wire (or 15 amp fuse wire)
2 wooden beads, 1cm (½in) across
strong glue
wire cutters or old scissors

For pierced ears

For unpierced ears

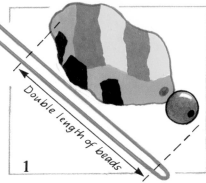

1 *Double length of beads*

You can make these earrings for either pierced or unpierced ears. Use clip-on attachments for unpierced ears and ear hooks for pierced ears.

First measure your beads. Double this measurement and add 5cm (2in). Use the wire cutters to cut two pieces of wire this long, one for each earring.

Making paper beads*

The quantities below will make three bracelets, two necklaces and a pair of earrings.

Six sheets of colored paper (such as cover paper), 52 × 78cm (20 × 30in), 150ml (¼pt) of wallpaper paste, an old dishpan, a 3¾mm** knitting needle, a thin paste brush, clear paper varnish, Vaseline and a ruler.

Making big, tapered beads

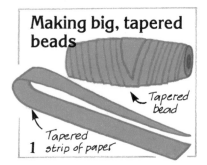

Tapered bead

1 *Tapered strip of paper*

Cut a strip of paper about 3cm × 78cm (1in × 30in). Then cut it to a point from half-way along, as shown. This makes it taper at each end.

2 *Wallpaper paste*

Coat a knitting needle with a thin layer of Vaseline. Then thinly brush some of the wallpaper paste over one side of the strip of paper.

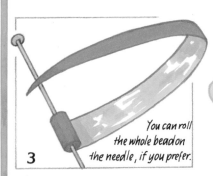

3 *You can roll the whole bead on the needle, if you prefer.*

Roll the strip around the knitting needle a few times to form a hole, then slip it off and roll by hand. Make all the beads like this.

Making small, straight beads

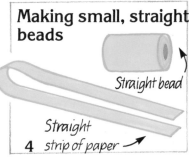

Straight bead

4 *Straight strip of paper*

Cut straight strips of paper 1½cm × 78 cm (½in × 30in). Then paste them, roll them up and varnish them, as for the big beads.

Varnishing both types of bead

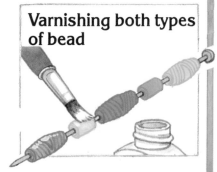

When the paste is dry, put the beads on to the knitting needle, five at a time and varnish them. Let the varnish dry, then varnish another batch.

* You can see how to adapt these beads on page 112. **English size 9, or US size 4.

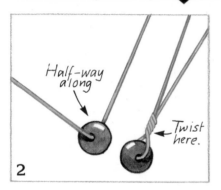

2
Push a small wooden bead to the middle of one of the lengths of wire. Bend both ends around the bead, and twist them together a few times.

3
Thread both ends of wire through your papier mâché bead. Then thread one end through the hole in the ear hook or clip, as shown above.

4
Wind the second end of wire around the first. Then dab a tiny blob of glue on the spare ends of wire and push them back into the earring.

Paper necklace and bracelet ▲▲ ●●

You will need :
For the necklace: 26 big rolled paper beads, OR 16 big and 16 small beads
about 1m (1yd) of elastic cord
paper varnish and varnish brush

For the bracelet: about 5 big beads and 3 or 4 small beads
about 25cm (10in) of elastic cord
paper varnish and varnish brush

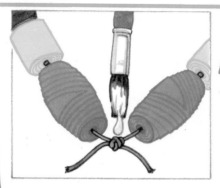

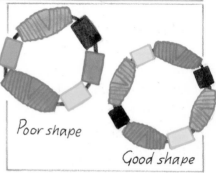

To make a necklace, thread the beads on to the elastic, varying the colors and sizes. Knot the elastic securely, then seal it with a blob of varnish. Trim ends.

You make the bracelet in the same way, but you need to arrange the beads evenly so that you end up with a good circular shape, as shown above.

Paper earrings ▲▲ ●●

You will need:
6 big paper beads and 2 small paper beads
4 wooden beads, 1cm (½ in) across
1 pair kidney wires or clips (with loops for dangly earrings)
2 lengths of 0·6mm (⅟₆₄ in) wire (or 5 amp fuse wire) 30cm (12in) long

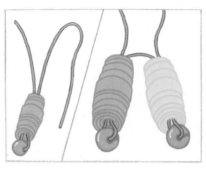

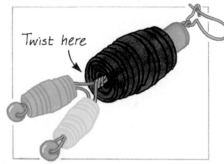

Thread a wooden bead, then a big bead half-way along the wire and thread one end back up the big bead. Thread on two more beads, as shown, doubling the wire through the big bead again.

Twist the wire at the top of the two big beads, then thread the double wire through a third big bead and a small bead. Thread on a kidney wire and finish as for the papier mâché earrings.

Natural things

The jewelry on the next four pages is all based on primitive shapes and natural, earthy colors. It is made from clay and wooden beads, corks, seeds and leather thongs. Clay beads are quite easy to make. Once you have mastered the basic techniques, you can experiment with different shapes and textures of bead. Combined with plain wooden beads and stained corks, they can look very dramatic.

In this section, you will see how to make the items of jewelry shown here.

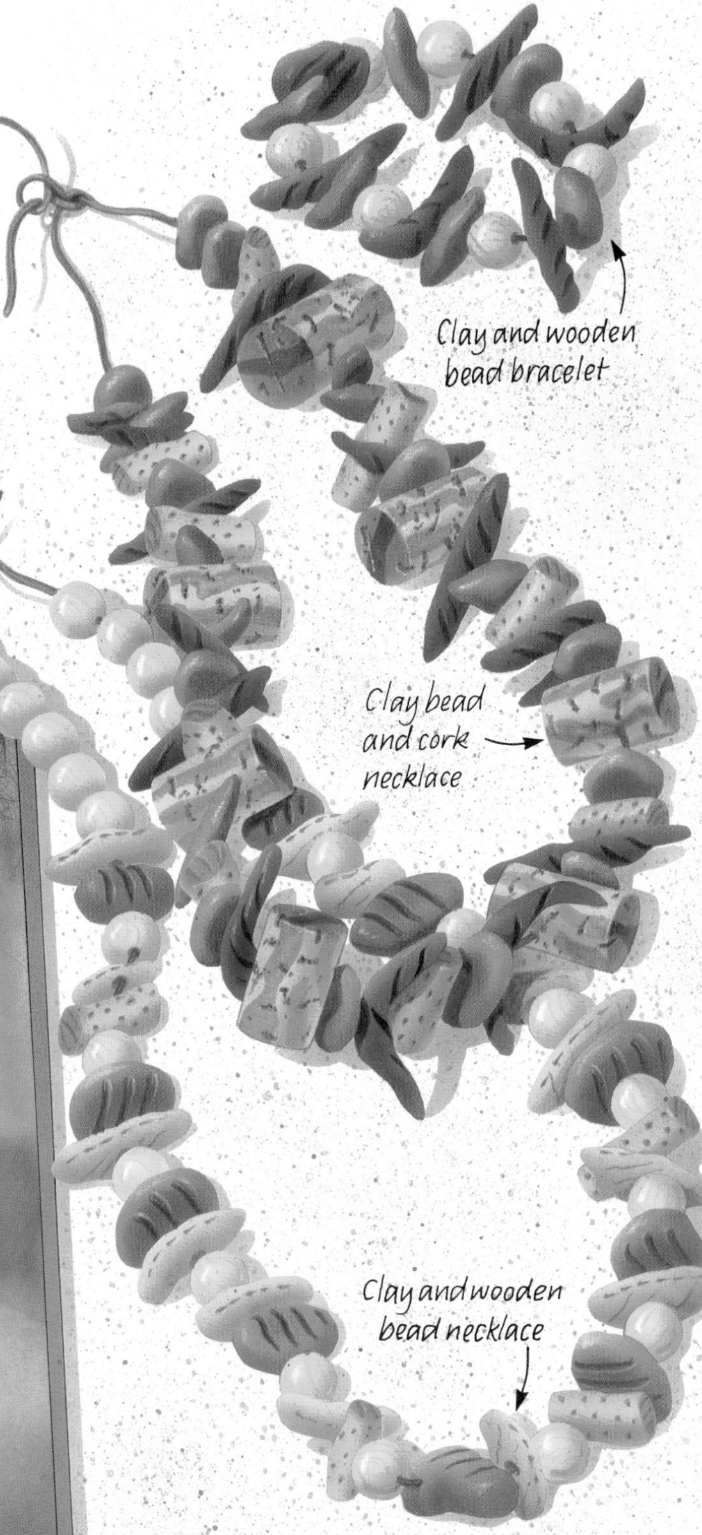

Clay and wooden bead bracelet

Sunflower seed earrings

Clay bead and cork necklace

Clay and wooden bead necklace

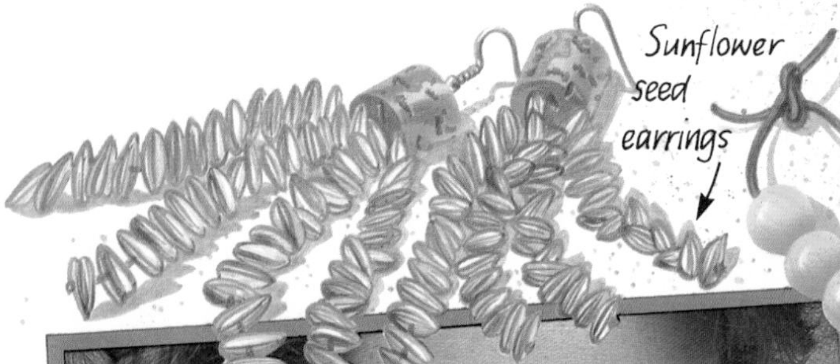

Natural look make-up looks very good with this jewelry. See page 82 to find out how to put it on.

About self-hardening clay

You can buy self-hardening clay from most craft shops. Some makes come in a range of different colors*, others come in just one color and can be painted afterwards. Self-hardening clay is easy to mold and dries to a hard, smooth finish when baked in the oven. Read the instructions on the package before you begin.

Different shapes of bead

Below are the various designs of bead used for the jewelry shown opposite. You can design your own beads if you prefer, making patterns with implements such as clay modelling tools, coins with serrated edges, or pencils.

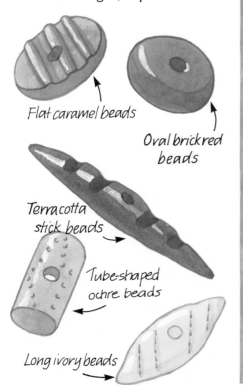

Flat caramel beads

Oval brick red beads

Terracotta stick beads

Tube-shaped ochre beads

Long ivory beads

Making clay beads

You will need seven packages of clay in different colors to make all the jewelry in this section. Choose earthy colors such as terracotta, ivory and ochre, for a natural look.

You will also need a 4mm** knitting needle, an old serrated knife and an old fork, clay varnish, a baking tray and some foil.

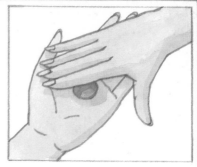

Roll a small piece of clay in your hands until it is soft. Then mold it into a bead. There are some ideas for bead shapes on the left.

The serrated edge makes a good pattern.

Gently pierce the center of the bead with your knitting needle. Before taking it off, mark patterns on it with the knife blade or fork prongs.

For the flat, caramel beads only, carve a pattern first, using the prongs of the fork. Then pierce the center of the bead with the knitting needle.

Check oven temperature given on the package.

Cover a baking tray in foil. Space the beads out on it. Heat the oven to 100-130°C (200-250°F) and bake for 10-20 minutes.

When the beads are cool, varnish them, letting one side dry before doing the other. On page 108 you can see what you can make with the beads.

---

*E.g. *Fimo*. See addresses on page 127   **English size 8, and US size 5.   107

Natural things 2

Clay bead and cork necklace ▲▲▲ ●●

You will need:
1 package of brick red clay
1 package of terracotta clay
½ package of ochre clay
7 new wine bottle corks*
bottle of wood stain
  and fine paint brush
clay varnish and varnish brush
1m (1 yd) leather thonging
old serrated knife
old fork
pointed skewer
baking tray and foil

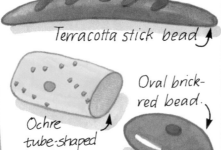

Terracotta stick bead

Ochre tube-shaped bead

Oval brick-red bead.

First make 17 oval brick red beads, 18 terracotta stick beads and 8 tube-shaped ochre beads, following the instructions on the previous page.

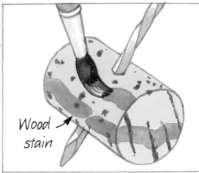

Wood stain

Carefully pierce the corks horizontally with the skewer, as shown. Paint on the wood stain in wavy lines. Leave the corks to dry, then varnish them.

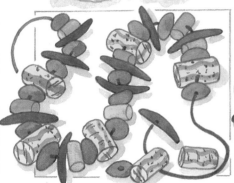

When the varnish is dry, thread the corks and the clay beads on to the thonging. Arrange the corks near the front, to give your necklace a good shape.

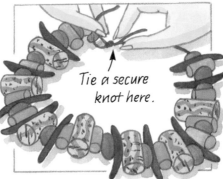

Tie a secure knot here.

Check your finished necklace for length. If it is too long, take off some of the beads from each end. Finally, tie the thonging in a secure knot.

Design hint

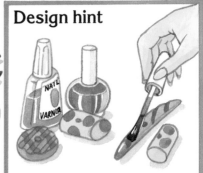

You could use nail varnish to paint patterns on your beads. You do not need to varnish them again if you decide to do this.

Clay and wooden bead bracelet ▲▲▲ ●●●

You will need:
7 wooden beads about 2cm
  (¾ in) across
½ package of brick red clay
½ package of terracotta clay
about 22 cm (9 in) of
  elastic cord
clay varnish and varnish brush
baking tray and foil
4 mm knitting needle
old serrated knife
old fork

Stretch elastic to seal knot.

Make six oval brick red beads and six terracotta stick beads (turn to page 107 to see how). Thread them on the elastic, knot it, then seal it with varnish.

Some finished bracelets.

*You can buy these from shops selling home-made wine kits and from drugstores.

Sunflower seed earrings ▲ ●

You will need:
100g (4oz) sunflower seeds
1 spool grey button thread
sewing needle
2 new wine corks
1 bottle of wood stain
fine paint brush
1 pair ball hooks or clips (with loops for dangly earrings)
sharp knife
pointed skewer
old towel or rag
varnish and varnish brush

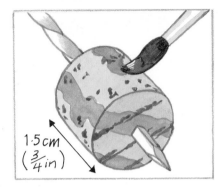

1·5 cm (¾ in)

Cut a piece of cork, 1½cm (¾in) deep. Pierce it vertically, as shown, then paint on some wood stain. Soak the seeds in water for an hour.*

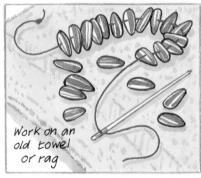

Work on an old towel or rag

Drain the seeds. Then knot one end of a piece of thread. Thread 22 seeds on to it, then thread it through the cork and cut it off 15cm (6in) from the top.

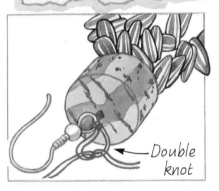

Double knot

Repeat with three more strands, threading them through the same piece of cork. Tie the strands on to the earring wire in a double knot.

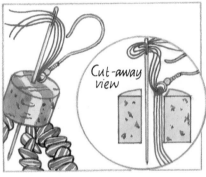

Cut-away view

Thread each end on to a needle and push them into the cork, as shown. Seal the knot above the cork and the knots at the base of each strand with varnish.

A finished pair of earrings

Clay and wooden bead necklace ▲▲▲ ●●●●

You will need:
1 package ivory clay
1 package caramel clay
½ package ochre clay
25 wooden beads, about 2cm (¾in) across
1m (1yd) leather thonging
clay varnish and varnish brush
4mm knitting needle
old serrated knife
old fork
baking tray and foil

Make 13 long ivory beads, 5 flat caramel beads and 5 ochre tube-shaped beads (see page 107). Thread them on to your thonging starting with six wooden beads.**

Finish off with six wooden beads. Adjust the length of your necklace by taking off some of the wooden beads at each end, if it is too long. Tie the thonging in a knot.

*So that they do not crack when threaded.   **This makes the necklace more comfortable to wear.   109

Pretty things

On the next six pages you can find out how to use rolled paper beads, ribbon-type yarn, fabric flowers, marabou and colored clay to make a collection of delicate jewelry in soft pastel shades.

In this section, you will find out how to make the items shown below.

Multi-strand necklace

Rose brooch

Rose brooch

Floral hair comb

Marabou earrings

Ribbon-covered bangles

Rose earrings

Ribbon-covered bangles ▲ ●●●

You will need:

50g (2oz) ball of ribbon-type yarn* (1 ball of yarn covers at least 3 bangles)
old plastic bangles ½cm (¼in) to 1cm (½in) thick and about 7cm (2¾in) in diameter
strong glue
small elastic band
scissors

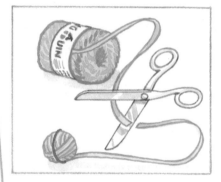

Cut about 3m (3½yd) of yarn off the main ball and wind it into a smaller ball. Unwind 30cm (1ft) of it to start with, and put an elastic band round the rest.

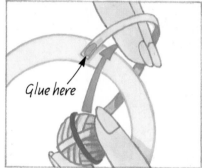

Glue the end of the yarn on to the bangle. Then take the yarn, in a loop, round the outside edge of the bangle and up the middle, as shown above.

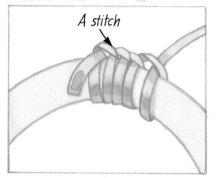

A stitch

Pass the ball of yarn through the loop and pull it until a stitch forms. Carry on like this, pushing each stitch close to the one before.

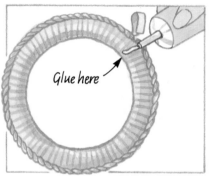

Glue here

When the whole bangle is completely covered, cut off the spare yarn, leaving a 1cm (½in) end. Glue this firmly to one side of the bangle.

Design hint

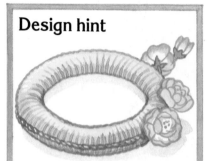

You can adapt the basic design to suit your taste. For example, you could glue a few fabric flowers on to the bangle. Then wind your yarn round to cover the stalks.

Floral hair comb ▲ ●●

You will need:

about 2m (2yd) ribbon-type yarn
plastic hair comb
strong glue
spray of small silk flowers**
scissors

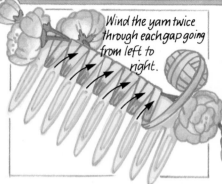

Wind the yarn twice through each gap going from left to right.

Glue flowers along the top, outside edge of the comb. Glue one end of the yarn to the back of the bar and wind it round, to cover the stalks, as shown.

Wind the yarn only once through each gap going from right to left.

Then wind the yarn back to the beginning again, diagonally, as shown, to cover any gaps. Cut off the spare yarn and glue the end to the back of the comb bar.

*Such as *Pingouin Ruban*.   **You can buy these from department stores.   111

Pretty things 2

Multi-strand necklace ▲▲▲ ●●●

You will need:

6 sheets strong white paper, about 30×20cm (12 × 8 in)

¼ liter (about ½ pt) wall paper paste and fine paste brush

paper varnish and varnish brush

poster paints and fine paint brush

toothpicks and Vaseline

3m (3½ yd) bead thread, sewing needle and screw clasp

88 glass beads ¾ cm (⅝ in) across

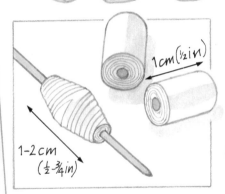

Cut the paper into 87 strips about 1cm (½in) x 30cm (1ft). Roll them into beads (see page 104) using a greased toothpick to form the hole.

Thin some poster paint with an equal amount of water and paint patterns on the rolled beads. Let each color dry before using another. Varnish them when dry*.

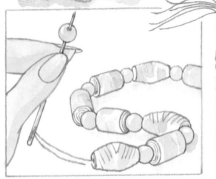

Thread the needle with 1m (40in) of thread. Working on a flat surface, so the beads stay on, thread 31 rolled beads on to it, alternately with 30 glass beads.

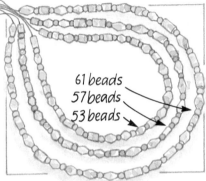

Make two more rows in the same way, using 29 paper beads and 28 glass beads for the middle one and 27 paper beads and 26 glass, for the short one.

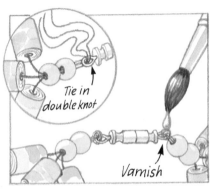

Thread two glass beads on to all three row ends. Then tie the ends on to one half of the clasp and varnish the knot to make it strong. Repeat at the other end.

Hoop earrings ▲▲ ●

You will need:

pair of silver earhoops 3½ cm (1½ in) across

4 glass beads (or more if you prefer) ¾ cm (⅝ in) across

2 rolled beads (or more if you prefer).

Paint and varnish the rolled paper beads, as for the necklace. Thread a glass bead, then a rolled bead, then another glass bead on to each earring.

Design hint

You can use any combination of beads, threaded on to the ear hoops. Try two paper beads and one glass bead, or just one big paper bead.

Marabou bangles ▲ ●●

You will need:

plastic bangle at least 8 cm (3 in) in diameter
about 1 m (1 yd) of marabou*
1 spool of matching thread
sewing needle
about 1 m (1 yd) ribbon-type yarn (or ribbon ½ cm [¼ in] wide)
strong glue
scissors

Glue one end of the marabou to the bangle. Bind it with thread, as shown. Wind the marabou evenly around the bangle and secure the other end as before.

Glue one end of your yarn to the bangle and wind it tightly round the join, until it is all used up. Glue the end neatly in place on the inside of the bangle.

Glue end here

Marabou Earrings ▲ ●●

You will need:

2 wooden curtain rings 6 cm (2½ in) across, with eyelets
8 m (9 yd) ribbon-type yarn (or ribbon ½ cm [¼ in] wide) cut into 2 equal lengths
40 cm (16 in) marabou cut into 2 equal lengths
1 spool of matching thread
sewing needle
1 pair of kidney wires
strong glue

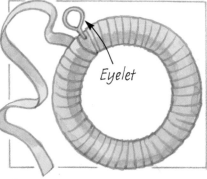

Eyelet

Glue one length of yarn next to the eyelet of one of the curtain rings. Wind the yarn tightly round the ring, as shown. Leave 15 cm (6 in) free at the end.

Bind together the ends of a piece of marabou with thread. Then glue it on to your curtain ring, so the join aligns with the neck of the eyelet.

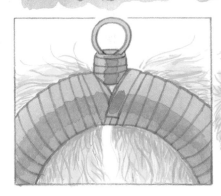

Wind the spare 15 cm (6 in) of yarn around the neck of the eyelet to cover the join, then around the curtain ring. Glue the end to the back of the ring.

Pull the marabou loop through to the front of the curtain ring and fluff it up. Thread the ring on to your earring wire. Repeat for the other earring.

This jewelry looks good worn with a fluffy jumper.

*Marabou is stork's down. You can buy it from notions departments and department stores.

Pretty things 3

Rose brooches and earrings

You can make these delicate rose brooches and earrings from self-hardening clay.* The ones shown here were made using clay which was already colored, but you can also buy a plain clay and paint and varnish it after baking. Use thinned poster paint and the varnish which the clay manufacturer recommends.

Posy and garland brooches.

Earrings.

Making the roses

Half a package each of pink, pale peach, green and yellow clay is enough to make all the things shown on these two pages. You could use what is left over to design your own rose jewelry.

The roses are made up from flowers, buds and leaves. They are time-consuming to make but the results are well worth the effort.

Bud

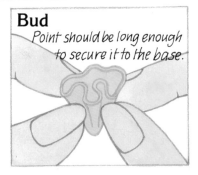

Point should be long enough to secure it to the base.

Make a small ball of peach clay, then flatten it into a disc about 1mm (1/16in) thick. Gently pinch the center into a point.

Leaf

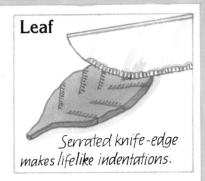

Serrated knife-edge makes lifelike indentations.

Roll out some green clay about 1mm (1/16in) thick. Use your knife to cut out a leaf about 2½cm (1in) long. Mark it with the knife, as shown.

Flower

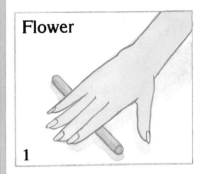

1

Break off a small piece of pink clay and mold it until it is soft. Roll it into a sausage about ½cm (¼in) wide and 12cm (5in) long.

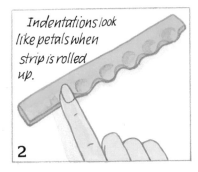

Indentations look like petals when strip is rolled up.

2

Flatten the sausage to make a strip about 1cm (½in) wide. Indent the edges with your fingertip, as above, to make the petals.

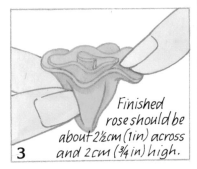

Finished rose should be about 2½cm (1in) across and 2cm (¾in) high.

3

Gently roll up the strip of clay, pinching one edge and opening out the other, to make a rose. Put a dot of yellow clay in the center.

* You can find out more about self-hardening clay on page 107.

Clip-on earrings

You will need:

self-hardening clay in pink, pale peach, green and yellow
baking tray and foil
old rolling pin
old serrated knife
clay varnish and varnish brush (optional)
2 clip-on earring backs
strong glue
sharp knife

Make two flowers, two buds and six leaves. Then make two discs, 2mm (⅛in) thick, which will cover your earring clips. Gently press the roses on to them.

Bake the earrings, as it tells you on the package. For a shiny effect, varnish the tips of the petals, when they are cool. Then glue on the earring backs.

Brooches

You will need:

self-hardening clay in pink, pale peach, yellow and green
old rolling pin
old serrated knife
baking tray and foil
clay varnish and varnish brush (optional)
brooch pins
strong glue
sharp knife

Posy brooch

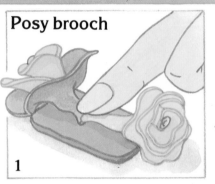

1

Make three flowers, two buds and seven leaves. Make a base about 4cm × 3cm × ½cm (1½in × 1¼in × ¼in). Gently press the roses on to it, as shown.

2

Bake the brooch, as it tells you on the package. When it is cool, varnish the tips of the petals if you want a shiny effect. Then glue on the brooch pin.

Garland brooch

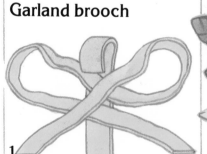

1

Cut a strip of clay ¼cm × 19cm (⅛in × 7½in). Make it into a figure of eight. Cut a strip 4cm (1½in) long and wrap it around the first, to make a bow.

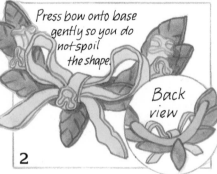

Press bow onto base gently so you do not spoil the shape.

Back view

2

Roll a V-shaped base. Make five buds and eight leaves and press them on to it, with the bow in the middle, as shown. Finish off as for the posy brooch.

Design hint

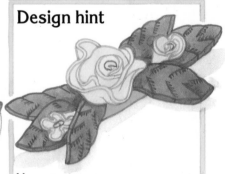

You can use any arrangement of roses that you wish, and vary the size of the base. The brooch above is made on a long, narrow base.

Classic things

The jewelry in this section is sophisticated and stylish. You can see how, with a coat of paint, old beads and bangles can be transformed into dazzling jewelry. You can also find out how to make glamorous jewelry out of clay and rhinestones and how to make some stunning party earrings from glittery net.

Here are some of the items in this section.

Net earrings

Enamel-painted necklaces

Button clip-on earrings

Enamel-painted bangles

This jewelry looks good worn with a simple crew or polo neck sweater.

Net earrings for pierced ears ▲ ●

You will need:
20cm (8in) glitter-patterned net
1 spool of strong, matching sewing thread
sewing needle
1 pair ball hooks
2 beads about 2cm (¾in) across
4 beads about 1cm (½in) across
4 gold washers about 1cm (½in) across
sharp scissors

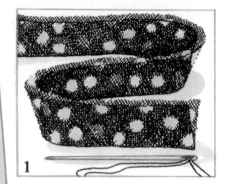

1

Cut the net into two strips 10cm (4in) × the width of the net*. Fold one strip in half lengthwise. Thread your needle with a double length of thread.

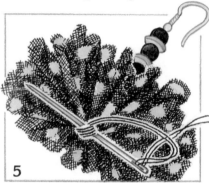

Make the stitches quite small.

2

Starting with a few stitches on top of one another, loosely sew along the fold, through both layers of net. Pull the thread end so the net begins to gather.

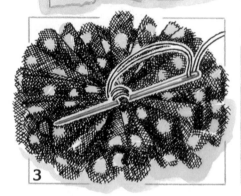

3

Gather the net up until the ends overlap to make a circle. Then sew across the center to close up the hole. Leave 20cm (8in) of spare thread on the needle.

Ball hook

4

On to the spare thread, thread a large bead, then three small beads alternately with two washers. Finally, thread on your ball hook.

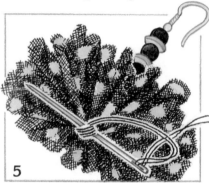

5

Now thread the needle back through each bead and washer to the under-side of the net and oversew to fasten off. Make a second earring in the same way.

Net clip-on earrings ▲ ●

You will need:
20cm (8in) glitter-patterned net
1 spool strong, matching sewing thread
sewing needle
sharp scissors
2 clip-on earring backs
strong glue

Make two net circles, as above. Fasten off neatly on one side of each circle. Then firmly glue an earring clip in the center of each one to cover the stitching.

Design hint

You could make either type of earring from plain net, and then decorate them, by glueing or sewing on sequins or tiny beads.

*If your net is very stiff, you may need to use less than the full width of the fabric.

Classic things 2

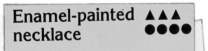

Enamel-painted necklace ▲▲▲ ●●●●

You will need:
37 beads about 2cm (¾in) across and 38 flat beads* about 1cm (½in) across
3m (3½yd) strong bead thread and darning needle
2 pots contrasting enamel paint, fine paint brush, turpentine, jar, and old newspapers clear varnish and varnish brush
2 pairs 2¼mm knitting needles**
transparent tape and a potato.

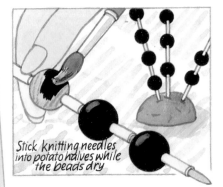

Stick knitting needles into potato halves while the beads dry

Thread the large beads on to knitting needles. Wind the tape in between. Holding each knitting needle over newspaper, paint the beads all over.

When this coat of paint is dry (after about six hours), paint patterns on the beads in the contrasting colored enamel. Leave to dry as before.

On to a double length of knotted thread, thread a flat bead, then a round one, then another flat one. Continue until all the beads are used up.

Varnish here

Tie the ends of the thread together in several double knots and cut off any left-over thread. Seal the knots with a blob of varnish.

Design hint

This necklace looks good in any colors. You could paint an old bangle to match it and make some earrings (see below) for a matching set.

Button clip-on earrings ▲▲▲ ●●

You will need:
2 round buttons about 2½cm (1in) across, with metal shanks
pliers
2 pots contrasting enamel paint, fine paint brush, turpentine jar, and old newspapers
1 pair clip-on earring backs
strong glue

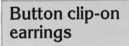

Shank

Twist the shank of the button with the pliers until it breaks off. Repeat with the other button. Working on newspaper, paint both buttons all over.

Earring back

Leave the buttons to dry for six hours. Then paint patterns on the front of the buttons, in a contasting paint color. When dry, glue on the earring backs.

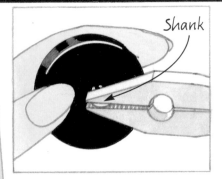

*You could use small buttons instead.   **English size 13, US size 0.

Speckled necklace ▲▲▲▲ ●●●

You will need :
300 beads about 1cm (½ in) across
2 pots contrasting enamel paint,
  fine paint brush, turpentine,
  jar and old newspapers
stiff bristled paste brush
2 x 4 row end bars
3m (3½ yd) strong bead thread,
  1 spool of ordinary sewing thread
  and sewing needle
pliers and scissors
strong glue
  jump ring and bolt ring

Before you start

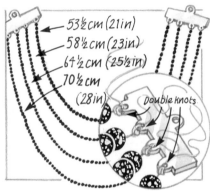

The jewelry on this page is patterned by splattering it with white paint. This is fun to do, but can be rather messy so it is best to do it out of doors, on a fine day, or in a garage or workroom. You should put down lots of old newspaper first.

You might have to re-touch patchy areas later

Thread the beads loosely on ordinary thread*. Then paint them on one side with your base color. When dry, turn them over and paint the other side.

Stiff bristled paste brush

Mix some contrasting paint with an equal amount of turpentine in a jar. Splatter your beads with it, as shown. Leave them to dry. Turn them over and repeat.

53½cm (21in)
58½cm (23in)
64½cm (25½in)
70½cm (28in)
Double knots

Thread your needle with bead thread and make up four rows of beads the above lengths. Tie the ends to the loops of the end bars, as shown.

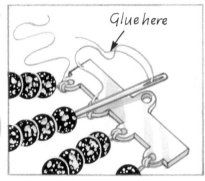

Glue here

Rethread the needle. Run glue along the thread and push it back through a few beads to secure it. Repeat for each strand at either end.

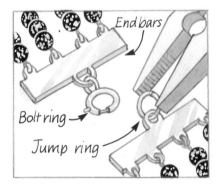

End bars
Bolt ring
Jump ring

Using pliers to open and close them, fit a jump ring through the loop on one end bar and a bolt ring through the loop on the other one.

Design hint

You can decorate a bangle to match this necklace, and make some matching button earrings (see left) which can be splattered in the same way.

Speckled jewelry

*If you rest them on a flat surface, they won't fall off as you thread them.

Classic things 3

About rhinestones*

Rhinestones without mounts   Mounts   Rhinestones with mounts

Imitation jewels made of glass or plastic are called rhinestones. Some have metal mounts which you can either clip on to the back of the stone, or use separately for extra decoration.

Rhinestone brooch ▲ ●●●●

You will need:

about ½ package self-hardening clay
baking tray and foil
tweezers
ruler
sheets of clean, white paper
brooch back
rhinestones for decoration
strong glue

Roll a ball of clay 4cm (1½in) across. Working on clean paper, flatten it into a disc about 6cm (2½in) across and ½cm (¼in) thick, using a ruler**.

Use tweezers to arrange the rhinestones on the brooch, as shown. Then gently press them into the clay with your finger tip, without touching the clay.

Put the brooch on your baking tray and bake it in the oven, following the instructions on the packet of clay. When it is cool, glue on a brooch back.

Design hint

Initial brooch   Small brooch

You can make brooches in practically any shape and size and vary the patterns you make with the rhinestones.

Rhinestone key-ring ▲ ●●●

You will need:

about ¼ package of self-hardening clay
ruler
sheet of clean, white paper to work on
baking tray and foil
rhinestones and mounts
tweezers
key-ring fixture

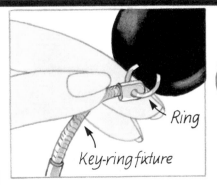

Ring

Key-ring fixture

Roll a ball of clay about 2½cm (1in) across. Push the key-ring fixture firmly into it as shown, so that the ring is half buried in the clay.

Flatten the ball into a disc about 4½cm (1¾in) across. Then decorate it with rhinestones and mounts, and bake it, as for the brooch above.

* See page 127 for addresses of suppliers.   **This is to avoid finger marks in the clay.

Rhinestone cuff-links ▲ ●●●

You will need:

about ¼ package of self-hardening clay
ruler
sheet of clean, white paper to work on
baking tray and foil
pair of cuff-link backs
rhinestones and mounts
tweezers

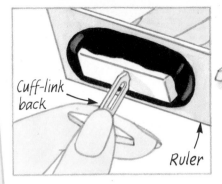

Cuff-link back

Ruler

Roll a piece of clay the size and shape of your cuff-link back. Flatten it with a ruler on to the cuff-link back, so it extends ¼cm (⅛in) all round.

Make the other cuff-link in the same way. Decorate both of them with rhinestones and rhinestone mounts and bake them, as for the brooch opposite.

Rhinestone rings ▲ ●●●

You will need:

about ½ package self-hardening clay (makes two or three rings)
baking tray and foil
ruler
sheet of white paper to work on
flat-ring backs
rhinestones and rhinestone mounts for decoration
strong glue

Designing a round, flat ring

Rhinestone mounts

Roll a ball of clay 1½cm (¾in) across. Flatten it with a ruler into a disc about 2cm (1in) across and ½cm (¼in) thick. Decorate it as for the brooch.

Designing a dome-shaped ring

Back flattened with ruler

Roll an oval piece of clay about 2cm (1in) long and 1cm (½in) high. Flatten one side of it with a ruler. Decorate it as for the brooch opposite.

Finishing the rings

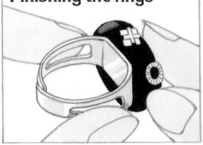

Bake the decorated clay in the oven, following the instructions on the packet. When it is cool, glue the clay on to the ring backs, as shown.

Design hint

Instead of using a flat ring back, you could mount the round, flat ring on a claw-shaped ring back, so that the tips of the claws stick out round the edge.

Rhinestone jewelry.

Crazy things

The jewelry in this section is bright and fun to wear. You can find out how to make woolly pom poms with left-over yarn, and adapt them to make various kinds of jewelry.

There are also lots of ideas for making crazy jewelry out of children's toys.

Here are some of the things you will find on the next three pages.

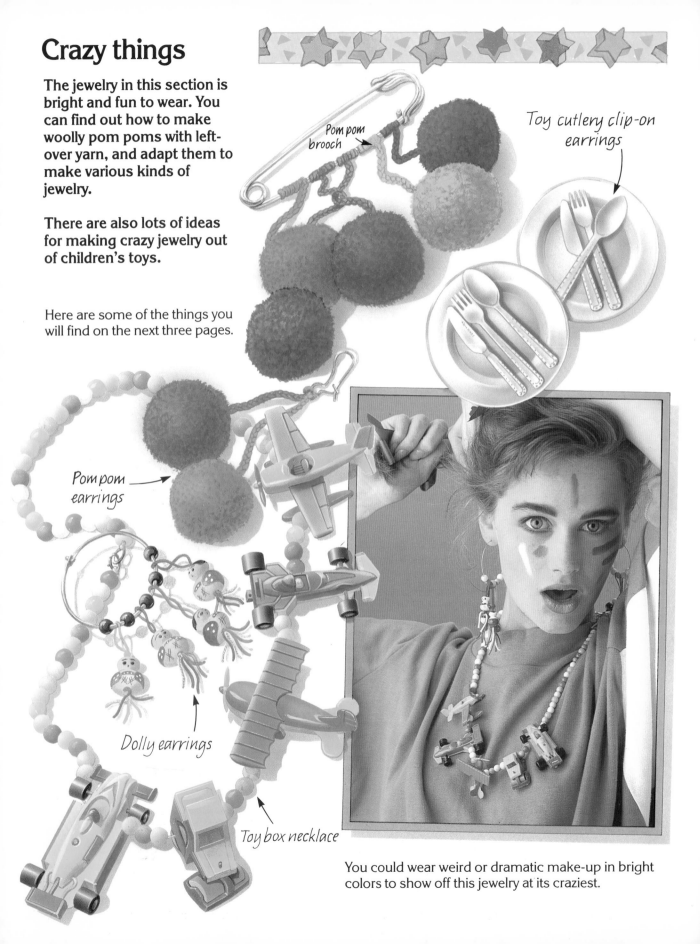

Pom pom brooch

Toy cutlery clip-on earrings

Pom pom earrings

Dolly earrings

Toy box necklace

You could wear weird or dramatic make-up in bright colors to show off this jewelry at its craziest.

Toy box necklace

You will need:

5 plastic toys such as miniature cars, trains and planes, plastic animals, dolls house furniture etc

82 plastic beads about 1cm (½in) across

about 1½m (5ft) strong bead thread

sewing needle

jump ring and bolt ring

scissors

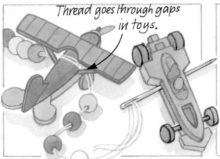

Thread goes through gaps in toys.

Thread your needle with double thread. Leaving 10cm (4in) at the start, thread on 33 beads*. Thread the toys, with about four beads between each one.

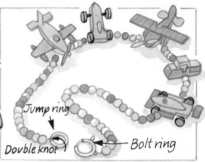

Jump ring

Double knot

Bolt ring

Thread 33 more beads, leaving 10cm (4in) of thread at the end. Tie on a bolt ring at one end and a jump ring at the other and trim off the spare thread.

Cutlery brooch and clip-on earrings

You will need:

3 sets of miniature plastic or metal cutlery and plates**

strong glue

clip-on earring backs

brooch back

scrap paper to work on

Glue cutlery where you like

Glue the cutlery firmly on to the plates. Glue earring clips on to the backs of two plates and a brooch back on to the back of a third and leave them to dry.

Cutlery earrings and brooch.

Dolly earrings

You will need:

1 pair of ear hoops about 3½cm (1½in) across

8 little wooden dolls (or Christmas decorations) with hanging loops

10 plastic beads about 1cm (½in) across

Thread up four wooden dolls (or Christmas decorations) on each ear hoop, alternately with five plastic beads. Start and finish with a bead.

Design hint

Pearl and pig necklace

Doll's shoe brooch

You can use all sorts of things to design your own crazy jewelry. The basic techniques stay the same. Above are some ideas.

*Work on a flat surface so the beads stay on the thread.   **You can buy these from some toy shops.

Crazy things 2

Making a woolly pom pom and chain

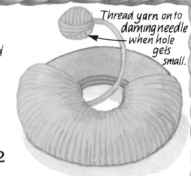

Dotted lines show how to find center of card square.

Thread yarn on to darning needle when hole gets small.

1

2

You need spare double knitting yarn, a piece of card 7cm (3in) square, a pencil, sharp scissors, a crochet hook and a darning needle.

On double card, draw a 3½cm (1¼in)* diameter circle. Draw a 2cm (¾in) diameter circle in the middle of it. Cut them out to make two rings.

Wind your yarn into a ball which will fit through the center hole. Then tie the end on to the two rings and wind the yarn around them.

Loose slip knot

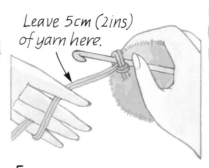

Leave 5cm (2ins) of yarn here.

3

4

5

When the hole is full, cut the yarn between the rings. Part them and tie a piece of yarn 75cm (30in) long, tightly around the middle.

Tear off the card rings and fluff out the pom pom. Tie a loose slip knot in the yarn ends, as close to the pom pom as you can make it.

Put your crochet hook through the slip knot as shown. Hold the crochet hook and pom pom in your right hand and the yarn, as shown, in your left.

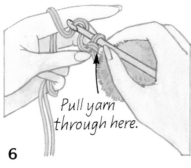

Pull yarn through here.

End loop. Pull to fasten off.

Design hint

6

7

Holding the slip knot in your left hand, catch a loop of double yarn with the crochet hook and draw it through the loop of your slip knot.

Carry on until the chain is the length you want it. Then hook the yarn through the end loop and pull tight. Leave the ends 18cm (7in) long.

You can make a two-tone pom pom. First work a few rounds of one color, then change to another color.

*You can make bigger or smaller pom poms by varying the size of your card rings.

Pom pom earrings ▲▲ ●

You will need:

2 pom poms with chains 5cm (2in) long

2 pom poms with chains 7cm (3in) long

scissors

darning needle

pair of kidney wires

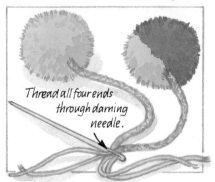

Make two pom poms with 5cm (2in) chains and two with 7cm (3in) chains. Thread the yarn ends of one long and one short chain on to a darning needle.

Thread all four ends through darning needle.

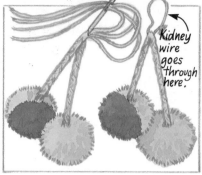

Kidney wire goes through here.

Neatly darn the four yarn ends into the chains, as shown. Thread a kidney wire through the join at the top. Make another earring in the same way.

Pom pom brooch ▲▲ ●

You will need:

5 pom poms with chains about 7cm (3in) long

darning needle

kilt pin* (or a giant safety pin) about 6cm (2½in) long

scissors

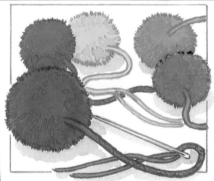

Make five pom poms, each with a chain about 7cm (3in) long. Thread the spare yarn at the ends of one chain on to your darning needle.

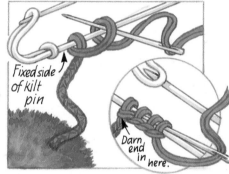

Fixed side of kilt pin

Darn end in here.

Stitch the yarn ends over the fixed side of the kilt pin. Then stitch for another 1cm (½in), as shown. To finish off, darn the ends into the crochet chain.

Repeat with the other four pom poms. When you have stitched them all on, the metal on the fixed side of the kilt pin should be covered with yarn.

Design hint

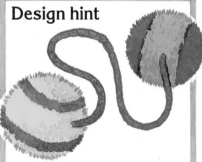

You can turn pom poms into almost anything. For instance you can make a hair bobble by stitching together two big pom poms on long chains.

The finished pom pom jewelry.

*A kilt pin is a giant safety pin. You can buy them from notions departments.

Tools, equipment and materials

Here you can find out about the things you need to make the jewelry. If you have problems finding the more unusual items, you may be able to order them by post. Many companies have a mail order service and there are some useful addresses opposite.

Findings

The metal components needed to make jewelry (known as findings) can be bought from specialist craft shops (see addresses opposite).

For earrings

Pierced ears:

Kidney wire

Metal ear hoop

Ball hook

Unpierced ears:

Clip (with loop for dangly earrings).

Screw (with loop for dangly earrings).

Clip-on earring back.

Screw-on earring back.

For necklaces

Screw clasp with loops.

Bolt ring and jump ring.

Jump ring and hook.

End bar.

For brooches

Brooch pin

Brooch back

For key-rings, cuff-links and rings

Cuff link backs

Ring backs

Key ring fixture

Wire (for earrings and bangles)

0.6mm ($^1/_{64}$in) wire (or 15 amp fuse wire) for earrings.

0.8mm ($^1/_{32}$in) wire (or 30 amp fuse wire) for papier mâché bangles.

Equipment

Jar		Turpentine	
Old rags		Newspapers	
Baking tray		Foil	
Cardboard box (to keep everything in).		Cardboard	
Old rolling pin		Transparent tape	
Old dishpan		Old spoon	

Tools

Ruler		Tape measure	
Wire cutters or blunt scissors		All purpose scissors	
Sharp knife		Small pliers	
Toothpicks		Knitting needles	
Sewing needles		Darning needle	
Paste brush		Fine paint brushes	
Varnish brush		Tweezers	
Pencil		Crochet hook	
Old serrated knife		Old fork	
Pointed skewer		Sandpaper	

Materials

Self-hardening clay (from art and craft shops).	**Strong paper,** such as coated cartridge, or cover paper (from art shops).	**Clear paper varnish** (from art shops). Alternatively, use clear nail polish.
Clay varnish (from art shops). Use the type recommended for the brand of clay you use.	**Wooden curtain rings** (from hardware or drapery departments).	**Buttons with shanks** (from notions departments).
Kilt pins (from notions departments).	**Ribbon-type yarn** (from wool shops). Sold under different brand names.	**Sequins** (from notions departments). These are shiny pieces of decorative plastic.
Rhinestones (from craft shops and notions departments).	**Marabou,** or stork's down (from notions departments).	**Fabric flowers** (from notions departments). Can be silk or synthetic.
Children's toys (from toy shops) and novelties from Christmas crackers.	**Old or broken jewelry**	**Plain or glitter-patterned net.** You can buy this from fabric shops.
Sunflower seeds (from health food stores and pet shops).	**Woodstain** (from hardware stores).	**Strong glue** which is recommended for wood, metal and plastic.
Poster paint and enamel paint	**Leftover yarn**	**Wine corks** (from shops stocking home wine-making kits).

Beads (from craft shops, notions departments and shops selling jewelry findings).

Plastic beads

Wooden beads   Metal washers   Glass beads

Thread (from notions departments and shops selling jewelry findings).

Elastic cord

Strong bead thread (polyester, or nylon)

Leather thonging   Thick metallic-cord

Useful addresses

Jewelry findings

Creative Beadcraft Ltd,
Unit 26, Chiltern Trading Estate,
Earl Howe Rd, Holmer Green,
High Wycombe,
Buckinghamshire, England.

Hobby Horse Ltd,
15-17 Langton Street, London
SW10 0JL, England.

Beadshop,
43 Neal Street, London
WC2H 9PJ, England.

Rio Grande Albuquerque,
6901 Washington NE,
Albuquerque,
New Mexico 87109, USA.

Watts International
Findings Company Inc.,
6024 South Memorial Drive,
Tulsa, Oklahoma 74145, USA.

John Bead Corporation Ltd,
21 Bertrand Avenue,
Scarborough, Ontario,
M1L 2P3, Canada.

Johnston Silvercraft Ltd,
579 Richmond Street West,
Toronto, Ontario,
M5V 1Y6, Canada.

Supercraft Emporium,
33 Moore Street, Perth, WA
6000, Australia.

Johnson Matthey Ltd,
114 Penrose Road,
Auckland 6, New Zealand.

Jewelcraft,
51 Unley Road, Parkside, 5063,
South Australia.

Fimo clay

Available from branches of
W.H. Smith in the UK.

For details of availability
elsewhere, please contact:

Staedtler (Pacific) Pty. Ltd,
P.O. Box 576, Dee Why, N.S.W.
2099, Australia.

Connelly Bros. Ltd,
7 Falcon Street, P.O. Box 496,
Parnell, Auckland 1, New
Zealand.

Accent Import Export Inc,
460 Summit Road, Walnut
Creek, Ca. 90210, U.S.A.

Dee's Delights Inc,
3150 State Line Road,
Cincinatti, North Bend, Ohio
45052, U.S.A.

Going further

If you would like to find out more about any aspect of jewelry, the books and addresses listed on this page will give you a good starting point.

Useful addresses

Australia

Australian Jewelers'
Association
46 Fullerton Road
Norwood
South Australia
5067

Manufacturing Jewelers' and
Silversmiths' Association
60 York Street
Sydney
New South Wales
2000

Queensland Jewelry
Workshop
P.O. Box 199
St Lucia
Queensland
4067

Canada

Canadian Jewelry
Association
1203,
20 Eglantine Avenue West
Toronto
Ontario
M4R IK8

New Zealand

Jewelers' and Watchmakers'
Association of New Zealand
P.O. Box 6549
Wellington

United States

Jewelers of America
1271 Avenue of the Americas
New York
NY 10020

Great Britain

National Association of
Goldsmiths
2 Carey Lane
London
EC2

School of Jewelry and
Silversmithing
City of Birmingham
Polytechnic
Vittoria Street
Birmingham
B1

British Jewelers'
Association
St Dunstans House
Carey Lane
London
EC2

Book list

Jewelry: general

Cartier, the Legend
Gilberte Gautier
Arlington

Gems and Jewels, a
Connoisseur's Guide
Benjamin Zucker
Thames and Hudson
(published in the US under the
imprint Thames and Hudson
Inc.)

The Illustrated Dictionary of
Jewelry
Harold Newman
Thames and Hudson
(published in the US under the
imprint Thames and Hudson
Inc.)

The Price Guide to Jewelry:
3000 BC – 1950 AD
Michael Poynder
Antique Collector's Club

Jewelry
David Marsh
Macmillan

Making Jewelry

The Encyclopaedia of Jewelry
Techniques
Peter Bagley
Batsford

Jewelry Concepts and
Technology
Oppi Untracht
Hale

The Techniques of Jewelry
Rod Edwards
Batsford

Selling jewelry

You may eventually want to try and make a living from making and selling jewelry. Many people do this by selling their work at craft fairs or to shops, for example.

The books below will help you find out more about setting up a business.

Usborne Introduction to
Business
Janet Cook
Usborne Publishing

Working for Yourself in the Arts and Crafts
Sarah Hosking
Kogan Page
(not available in the US or Canada)

PART FOUR

HAIR & HAIRSTYLING

Paula Woods

Edited by Felicity Everett
Designed by Nerissa Davies

Illustrated by Tessa Land, Peter Bull, Joanna Irving and Paul Sullivan

Photographs courtesy of Vidal Sassoon and The Kobal Collection

Additional designs by Christopher Gillingwater

Additional research by Sarah Caughlin

Contents

About hair and hairstyling

A new hairstyle can change your appearance radically. A successful one can improve your looks and lift your spirits. An unsuccessful one can make you reluctant to leave the house. Because of this, most people are prepared to spend quite large amounts of money having their hair done in a flattering style, and to devote the time to keeping it in good condition afterwards.

Part four is about choosing and looking after your hairstyle. It is also an introduction to hairdressing, for those with a passing interest in the tricks of the trade, or a serious ambition to become stylists themselves.

Pages 131-149 cover everything you need to know as a client, from choosing the right style to tips on looking after your hair on a daily basis and ways to vary your chosen style for a special occasion. This section of part four has a purple flash at the top of each page for easy reference.

Pages 150-175 are about the world of the professional hairstylist. This part tells you all about the equipment they need and gives a step-by-step guide to the basic cutting, perming and coloring techniques that a trainee hairdresser has to learn. This section has a green flash at the top of each page.

At the back of the book there is lots of down-to-earth careers advice on hairdressing and related fields. There is also some suggested reading and useful addresses, should you want to find out more about becoming a hairdresser.

How hair grows

The hair on your head is there for two reasons: to stop your body from losing heat, and to protect your scalp (and therefore your brain) from injury. Here you can find out about the structure of your scalp and hair.

Parts of the scalp

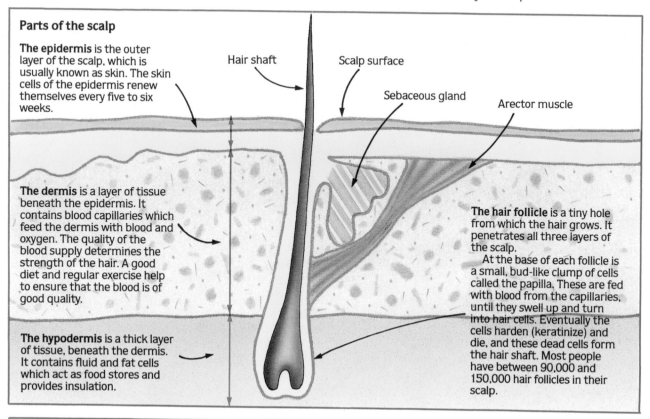

The epidermis is the outer layer of the scalp, which is usually known as skin. The skin cells of the epidermis renew themselves every five to six weeks.

Hair shaft

Scalp surface

Sebaceous gland

Arector muscle

The dermis is a layer of tissue beneath the epidermis. It contains blood capillaries which feed the dermis with blood and oxygen. The quality of the blood supply determines the strength of the hair. A good diet and regular exercise help to ensure that the blood is of good quality.

The hair follicle is a tiny hole from which the hair grows. It penetrates all three layers of the scalp.

At the base of each follicle is a small, bud-like clump of cells called the papilla. These are fed with blood from the capillaries, until they swell up and turn into hair cells. Eventually the cells harden (keratinize) and die, and these dead cells form the hair shaft. Most people have between 90,000 and 150,000 hair follicles in their scalp.

The hypodermis is a thick layer of tissue, beneath the dermis. It contains fluid and fat cells which act as food stores and provides insulation.

Cross section of a hair shaft

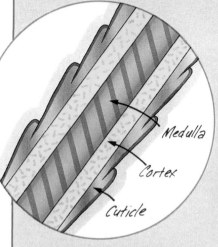

Medulla

Cortex

Cuticle

A hair shaft consists of three layers:

The medulla is the core of the hair shaft. It is a soft, spongy layer of round cells. The size of these cells determines the thickness of your hair.

The cortex is an inner layer made up of cells which give the hair elasticity and strength. It also contains a pigment* called melanin, which gives the hair its color.

The cuticle is a protective coating made up of clear, overlapping scales of keratin (a horn like substance). If you look after your hair, these scales should lie flat, making the surface of the hair look glossy.

The life cycle of a hair

Each hair lives between one and six years. It then dies and falls out of the hair follicle (see above).

Every day, between 50 and 150 hairs die, but new ones are constantly growing to take their place, so the hair loss is not noticeable.

There are three phases in the life cycle of a hair: the anogen phase, the telogen phase and the catogen phase. You can find out more about them on the right.

The **anogen phase** is the period of new growth. Most people's hair grows at a rate of about 1.3cm a month. The sebaceous glands are active throughout this phase. At any one time, 18% of your hair is in the anogen phase.

During the **telogen phase** growth stops and the sebaceous glands become less active. Only 1% of your hair is at this stage at any one time.

The **catogen phase** is the final one. The sebaceous glands stop working and the follicle shrinks. After about three months, the hair falls out. About 4 to 14% of hair is at this stage at any one time.

Pigment is a special name for the chemicals which give color to your hair and skin.

Hair types

Before styling your hair, a good hairdresser will examine it carefully to see what type it is. For example, how thick is it? What is its natural color? Is it greasy or dry? Doing this helps the hairdresser to make the most of your hair.

Below you can see why people have such different types of hair.

Thick or thin?

The thickness of your hair depends on the number of hair follicles* you have and how large each individual follicle is.

Blonds have the most hair follicles but because each hair is so fine, they appear to have the thinnest hair. Redheads, on the other hand, have the fewest hair follicles but owing to the thickness of each hair, they seem to have a lot of hair.

Hair color

The color of your hair is determined by a colored substance (called a pigment) within each hair shaft*. If you look closely you will see that although your hair has an overall shade, the individual hairs vary quite considerably.
You can change your natural shade by using a colorant (see pages 162-163). It is a good idea to choose a shade which is fairly close to your own, as this will probably suit your skin tone best.

Hair length

Whether or not you can wear your hair long depends on its growth rate and resilience. On average, each hair grows 1.3cm per month and continues growing for between two and six years. After this it falls out.

If your hair grows at an above average rate for five years or more, you will be able to choose a long hairstyle. If you have slow-growing or weak hair, you will probably not be able to grow it past your shoulders.

Hair follicles

As explained on page 131, your hair grows from tiny holes in your head, called follicles. The shape of these holes effect how curly your hair is. Their size determines whether it is thick or thin.

Small follicles

Small follicles produce fine hair. if you have fine hair, avoid rich conditioners as these make it soft and limp. To add body to your hair, try having it permed (see pages 166-167).

Large follicles

Large follicles result in thick hair. This can be stubborn to style and takes a long time to dry, but has the advantage of natural body.

See page 131 for more about hair follicles and hair shafts.

Round follicles

A round follicle produces straight hair. You can curl it temporarily in various ways (see pages 164-165).

Asian hair will hold a perm better and for much longer than any other type of straight hair. This is because the cuticle (see right) is particularly strong and thick.

Kidney-shaped follicles

A kidney-shaped follicle makes the hair kink and appear curly or wavy. The more acute the shape, the curlier the hair. You can straighten curly hair using perming lotion (see page 166) or heated straighteners (see page 173).

Afro Caribbean hair not only grows from a kidney-shaped follicle, but each shaft is oval in shape rather than round. This combination produces tighter curls.

An advantage of Afro Caribbean hair is that the curls protect the head from the sun's rays by absorbing them at varying angles. However, they also allow moisture to escape and prevent the natural oil from coating the hair shaft, so the hair is very often dry.

Shiny hair

How shiny your hair is depends on how well each hair shaft is able to reflect light. By keeping your hair in good condition you will ensure that the protective coating (the cuticle) of each hair shaft lies flat, as shown on the right. This creates a smooth surface which reflects light well.

Healthy cuticle: Scales lie flat and overlap creating a smooth surface to reflect light.

Damaged cuticle: Scales are cracked and splayed and so absorb light.

Dry, greasy or normal?

Hair follicles contain sebaceous glands (see page 131) which produce oil to keep the hair healthy. However, some produce too much, or too little oil, which can lead to your hair becoming greasy or dry.

This chart will help you identify your particular hair condition, and provides tips on looking after it. For more advice on hair care, see page 145.

Hair condition	Appearance	Cause	Associated problems	Solution
Greasy	Hair becomes lank and dull after washing. Looks greasy.	Sebaceous glands are producing too much oil.	People with fine hair or oily skin are more likely to have greasy hair.	Wash frequently* with a very mild shampoo as extra oil attracts dirt.
Dry	Hair is hard to control and feels rough to the touch. Looks dull and brittle.	Sebaceous glands are not producing enough oil. Alternatively, hair has been damaged by careless treatment.	Split ends (see page 174) can be a problem. Dry hair is often accompanied by dry skin.	Use a rich, specially formulated shampoo. Condition after every wash.
Combin-ation	Hair appears oily at the top and dry at the ends. Scalp may feel dry and flaky.	Often due to over-use of heated styling appliances which dry out the ends of the hair.	The hair may suffer from dandruff (see page 174) and split ends.	Use a mild shampoo and apply a rich oil-based conditioner to the ends of the hair only.
Normal	Hair is shiny and easy to manage. Feels soft and smooth to the touch.	Sebaceous glands are producing the correct amount of oil.	None	Use a mild shampoo and a conditioning rinse if necessary.

Frequent washing does not make hair more oily if you wash it carefully and with the right products.

Natural hair preparations

For generations, people have used herbal products to enhance their hair and skin. There are now many specialist shops which stock these products. However, you don't need to spend a fortune on them: much of what you need, such as lemons, oil and vinegar, can be found in the kitchen cupboard.

Before trying anything new, remember that even mild products, if over-used, can harm your hair. However, natural preparations used every so often will improve your hair.

On the right you can find out the properties of the different natural ingredients. Below are some recipes for shampoos and conditioners.

Cider vinegar is a mild acid. As many hair products are slightly alkaline, a vinegar rinse can help correct the pH balance of your hair and scalp (see page 170). This gives the hair extra body and shine. After using vinegar, always rinse thoroughly to remove all traces of its distinctive smell.

Lemon juice closes the pores (tiny holes) in the scalp and helps smooth down the overlapping scales of the hair shaft (see page 133). This leaves the hair looking glossy and well cared for.

Mayonnaise combines the properties of eggs, oil and vinegar. Together they leave your hair beautifully conditioned and shiny.

Egg shampoo

1. Vigorously beat together the white and yolk of an egg in a mixing bowl.

2. Massage the mixture thoroughly into unwashed dry hair and leave for around five minutes.

3. Rinse your hair in *cool* water: the egg is likely to scramble if the water is too hot.

Egg conditioner

1. Separate the egg yolk from the white. Beat the yolk thoroughly: this makes it easier to apply.

2. Wash your hair, then dab on the yolk with a sponge. Comb through to distribute it evenly.

3. Leave for 20 minutes and then rinse your hair thoroughly in cool water. Style hair as normal.

Warm oil treatment

1. Gently warm two tablespoons of oil in a saucepan. Then carefully massage it into your hair.

2. Wrap a piece of plastic wrap around your hair, and seal the ends by scrunching them together.

3. Cover with a warm towel*, and leave on overnight. Shampoo and rinse thoroughly.

Mayonnaise conditioner

1. Mix a tablespoon of cider vinegar, an egg yolk and a pinch of sugar. Stir in eight tablespoons of olive oil.

2. Beat vigorously until the mixture becomes thick and creamy, then bottle it and store it in the fridge.

3. Apply the mayonnaise as you would a warm oil treatment** or use it instead of a conditioner.

*The heat from the towel causes moisture to build-up under the plastic wrap.
** Leave for at least 20 minutes before rinsing.

Olive oil coats the hair with a thin layer of oil. This smooths down the outer cuticles (see page 133), allowing the hair to reflect light more efficiently and appear healthy and shiny.

Eggs make excellent cleansers. They cling to the dirt and, when you rinse your hair, they drag it away with them. As eggs contain protein they also act as a conditioner, leaving dull, lifeless hair full of body and shine. After using an egg, you will need to rinse your hair more than once to remove all traces of it.

Common herbs and plants can be used to cure various problems and improve the condition of your hair. You can apply them in the form of an infusion (see below).

Astringents

Astringents such as lime, lemon and witch hazel help to close the pores in your scalp and stem the flow of natural oil. They are therefore particularly good for greasy hair.

To keep your hair free of grease in between washes, apply astringent to your scalp using cotton wool.

Quick rinses

Lemon rinse. Add four teaspoons of lemon juice to a bowl of cool water, and use as a final rinse.

Vinegar rinse. Add half a cup of cider vinegar to a litre of water and use as a final rinse.

Infusions

You can make a wide range of hair remedies by soaking herbs or plants in hot water. These are known as infusions. Natural infusions add body and shine to all hair types and also help keep your hair in excellent condition.

To make an infusion

1. Place 25g of your selected herbs (see the chart on the right) in a container, and pour over 300ml of boiling water.

2. Close the container and leave in a warm place for several hours. The longer the infusion is allowed to steep, the stronger the effect of your rinse. Then strain the liquid into an airtight jar.

3. Use the infusion as a final rinse or as a supplement to your shampoo or conditioner (add half of it to shampoo or a quarter to conditioner).

Herb/flower	Property
Camomile flowers	Lightens blond hair. Adds shine to dull hair.
Hollyhock flowers	Adds blueish tinge to white or grey hair.
Lavender	Removes excess oil.
Marigold petals	Soothes irritated scalps. Brightens red tones in auburn hair.
Nettles	Stimulates hair growth.
Parsley	Helps prevent dandruff.
Rosemary	Prevents static.
Sage	Darkens grey hair. Adds shine to dark hair.

Buying herbal products

If you do not want to make your own herbal remedies you could buy ready-made versions from pharmacies or health shops. Look out for the items described below.

Orris root

If you do not always have time to wash your hair, buy some powdered orris root. This makes an excellent dry shampoo. Brush a little through your hair to remove grease and stale smells. Keep brushing until all traces of the powder have gone.

Rhassoul mud

Rhassoul or Moroccan mud is powder which, when mixed with water, makes a good cleanser for greasy hair. You can also use it to treat dandruff. It is sometimes sold as a ready-made shampoo.

Henna wax

This is a colorless wax which makes an excellent conditioning treatment for all hair types. Mix the henna wax with hot water (as directed on the container) and massage into clean dry hair. Leave on for about 30 minutes, then rinse.

Healthy hair – inside and out

Keeping your hair in good condition is not just a matter of choosing the right shampoo. A good diet and plenty of exercise are essential to give your hair shine and vitality. It is also important to protect it from extremes of temperature, pollutants and so on. Here you can find out how to make sure your hair looks good all year round, indoors and out.

Health and diet

For your hair to stay healthy, your scalp must receive a regular supply of blood. This ensures that the sebaceous glands and hair follicles work efficiently. To help your circulation, take plenty of exercise and eat a balanced, nutritious diet.

A healthy diet should include:

Low fat proteins. These are found in white meat and fish.

Vitamins (A, B and C). Vitamin A is found in milk, butter, eggs and fresh fruit and vegetables. Wholefoods, such as oats and wheatgerm contain vitamin B. Raw vegetables, salads and fresh fruit are high in vitamin C.

Minerals (iron, calcium and salt). These are found in liver, kidneys and vegetables.

You can also take vitamin supplements:

★ Yeast extracts such as brewers' yeast (which come in tablet or powder form), zinc or vitamin A tablets will improve the overall condition of your hair.

★ Brewers' yeast may also help if you find you are losing more hair than normal.

★ A daily course of vitamin E oil capsules may help if your hair is dry and brittle.

★ Kelp is a seaweed rich in vitamins and minerals. A course of tablets will strengthen and improve the condition of your hair.

Summer hair care

Summer usually makes you feel cheerful and energetic, which is good for your general health and therefore your hair. However it is important to be aware of the potentially harmful effects of summer weather and activities.

Swimming

Swimming, whether in the sea or a swimming pool, can be damaging to your hair. If possible rinse your hair afterwards to remove any salt water or chlorine, both of which leave harmful deposits and spoil your hair's condition.

Summer breezes

Warm winds increase the drying effects of the sun. Sea breezes often contain grains of sand which tear your hair leaving it frizzy and unkempt. Hair gel or a scarf will give better protection than a sun hat, which is likely to blow off.

The sun

Exposure to the sun lightens most hair types. This can look very attractive with a tan. However, just as too much sun can damage your skin, your hair may also suffer from prolonged exposure. The natural moisture in your hair may evaporate leaving it dull, brittle and lifeless, and increasing the risk of split ends.

To protect your hair, comb through a protective gel or wax containing a sun-screen.

Alternatively, wear a sun hat or tie a light colored** scarf around your head.

Always re-apply gels and waxes after swimming.

Summer vacation checklist

* Ensure that your hair is in good condition by having split ends trimmed off. If you are having a re-style, choose a simple cut which requires little effort to keep looking good.

* A deep conditioning oil treatment before you go will help to counteract the drying effects of the elements.

* Avoid coloring your hair just before going on vacation. The sun combined with salt water or chlorine may distort the color.

* Avoid perming your hair just before going on vacation as the sun can damage chemically-treated hair.

* These are taken internally.
** Light colors will reflect the sun's rays.

Winter hair care

In winter, it is not only the weather which can cause problems for your hair but the constant changes in temperature as you move between the cold outdoors and warm indoors.

You should always wear a hat when skiing.

The cold

Severe cold and sudden changes in temperature can make your hair brittle and dry. Always wear a hat or scarf out of doors to protect your hair as well as to keep you warm.

The wind

If you let your hair blow loose in the winter wind, you may end up with dry hair which is prone to split ends. Long hair may also become tangled and you could harm it trying to comb out the knots. To protect it, wear it tied back or cover it with a hat or scarf.

Snow, rain and mist

Moisture in the air, in the form of rain, snow and mist can make your hair frizzy, lifeless and unmanageable. This is because it reduces the effectiveness of styling products, such as hairsprays and gels. It will also take the body and shape out of styled hair.

Whilst an umbrella will protect you from bad snow and rain showers, light drizzle and mist can be all-pervasive. It may well be a waste of time curling or straightening your hair in this weather.

Winter vacation checklist

* Make sure your hair is well-cut and in good condition, as for a summer vacation (see left).

* If you are going skiing, you may find that wearing a tight-fitting hat causes perspiration and makes your hair greasier than usual.

Pack a mild shampoo which you can use every day, if necessary

* Many winter vacation resorts offer saunas amongst their leisure facilities. Saunas have a drying effect on your hair, so always use a conditioner when you wash it.

City haircare

If you move to a large town or city you may find that you need to wash your hair more often. This is because of the additional dirt in the air. It is best to change to a mild or frequent-wash shampoo. You may also find your hair difficult to manage. This is due to pollution in the air which affects the acid balance* of your hair. There is little you can do to prevent this, although using a pH balanced shampoo and conditioning your hair regularly may help.

Protecting the environment

Many everyday styling products come in aerosol sprays. These harm the atmosphere because they contain chlorofluorocarbons (CFC's). When you use an aerosol spray you release these chemicals into the atmosphere. They slowly destroy the earth's ozone layer (the layer of gas which filters out ultra-violet radiation from the sun).

Many companies now produce pump-action sprays, which are an effective alternative.

Indoor hair care

Home comforts, such as central heating or artificially purified and softened water, make life more enjoyable, but can cause problems for your hair. You can find out what these are and how to tackle them below.

Heating

Most home heating systems, and central heating in particular, evaporate the moisture from the air. This has a drying effect on your hair. You can replace some of the air's moisture by placing a bowl of water in each room of the house. Make sure they cannot easily be knocked over.

Tap water

In hard-water areas the water supply is often supplemented with fluoride and chlorine which purifies and softens the water, but is bad for your hair. If there are such chemicals in your water, make sure you condition your hair after shampooing.

*See page 170.

Choosing the right style

Have you ever found a picture of a hairstyle you would like and taken it along to your hairdresser only to be advised against it? This may be because of your hair type and texture (see pages 132-133), but the hairdresser will also consider your face shape and features. A good hairdresser will help you choose a style which suits the way you look. This involves deciding which features to emphasize and which to disguise. On these two pages you can find out what shape your face is and which styles might suit you.

Over the page are some tips on emphasizing your best features and choosing a cut to suit your lifestyle.

Face shapes

Once you have identified the shape of your face using the method shown on the opposite page, you can work out what sort of style might suit you. Here are some tips for the six basic face shapes.

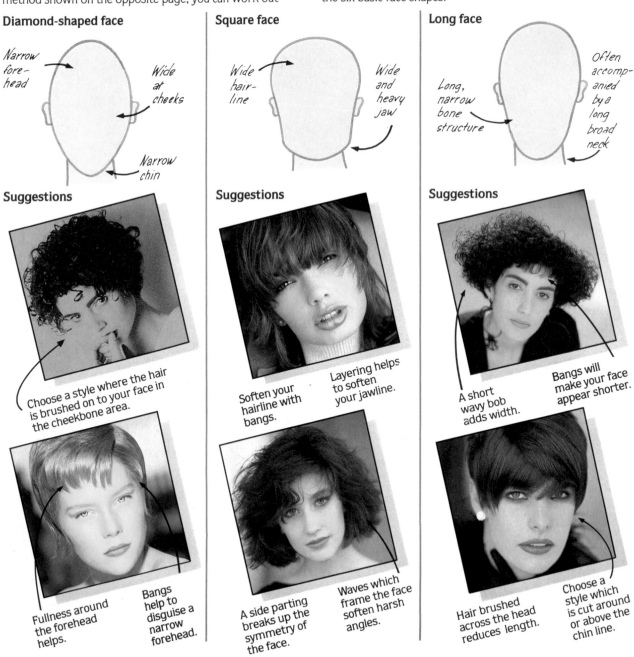

Diamond-shaped face

Narrow fore-head

Wide at cheeks

Narrow chin

Suggestions

Choose a style where the hair is brushed on to your face in the cheekbone area.

Fullness around the forehead helps.

Bangs help to disguise a narrow forehead.

Square face

Wide hair-line

Wide and heavy jaw

Suggestions

Soften your hairline with bangs.

Layering helps to soften your jawline.

A side parting breaks up the symmetry of the face.

Waves which frame the face soften harsh angles.

Long face

Long, narrow bone structure

Often accomp-anied by a long broad neck

Suggestions

A short wavy bob adds width.

Bangs will make your face appear shorter.

Hair brushed across the head reduces length.

Choose a style which is cut around or above the chin line.

What shape is your face?

To find out what shape your face is, measure it with a ruler, following the steps on the right. Write each measurement down and compare the results with the table provided.

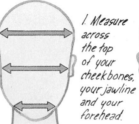

1. Measure across the top of your cheekbones, your jawline and your forehead.

2. Then measure from your hairline to your chin.

Oval	Length equal to one and a half times width.
Round	Almost as wide as it is long.
Long	Longer than it is wide.
Heart	Narrow at jawline, wide at forehead and cheekbones.
Square	Forehead, jawline and cheek-bones almost equal in width.
Diamond	Wide cheeks, narrow forehead and jawline.

Heart-shaped face

Wide fore-head

Wide at cheeks

Narrow chin

Suggestions

Avoid fullness near the cheeks.

Short cuts with fullness at the crown work well.

Bangs give balance.

A bob adds fullness around the jaw but lies flat against the cheeks.

Round face

Wide hair-line

Fullness at and below the cheekbones

Neck often seems short

Suggestions

Choose layered bangs rather than ones which are straight and heavy.

Short styles which give height work best.

Keep the sides of your hair short.

Use curls to create height, keeping the sides of your hair short.

Oval face

Neither too wide or too long

Jawline in propor-tion to forehead

Suggestions

Most styles flatter an oval face.

This style emphasizes the cheekbones.

You may be able to carry off an outrageous style, such as this one.

The varying angles and colors give the style great impact.

Most of us have an attractive feature which we would like to emphasize. Below you can find out how, by choosing the right style, you can make that feature a focal point.

Below you can found out how, with clever cutting and hairstyling, you can

play down less appealing prominent features.

Eyes. Choose a style where the hair is swept away from your forehead, as shown above.

Jawline. Choose a style that follows the line of your jaw. Fullness at the back will also emphasize your jawline.

Lips. A style where the hair is brushed on to your face will help to make your lips a focal point.

Cheekbones. Choose a style that follows the line of your cheekbones, as shown above.

Close-set eyes. A style where the hair is brushed on to your face around the eyes will reduce the area either side.

Short neck. A short, cropped style will make a short neck appear longer. Alternatively long hair worn up will have the same effect.

High forehead. A good way to disguise a high forehead is by choosing a style with sleek, straight bangs.

Deep-set eyes. Your eyes will look larger if you brush your hair up and away from your forehead in a style that is full around the temples.

Long neck. Wear your hair long to help to create the illusion of a shorter neck. If possible choose a curly style which will also add fullness.

Double chin. Keep the hair around your face above chin level to draw the eyes upwards. The back may be grown longer. A bob would be ideal.

Wearing glasses

If you wear glasses, make sure you take them to the hairdresser's with you. Then you can discuss with the hairdresser what style would complement your frames as well as your face as a whole.

If you wear your glasses all the time, then the hairdresser should ask you to put them on at different stages during your re-style. This ensures that the cut is not distorted when you wear your glasses.

Shorter styles that lie well above the ears allow your glasses to fit correctly.

Choose a style that lies well above or falls well below your ears. Haircuts in between tend to get caught underneath the glasses frames, or stick out at strange angles. It is also a good idea to avoid styles that have long bangs or that are brushed forward on to your face as these will get in the way of your glasses. If you have blond hair, delicate frames will probably suit you best. Bolder frames look good with darker hair.

Lifestyle

Your lifestyle is another important consideration when choosing a new hairstyle. However much you like a particular style, it is no use if it causes you practical problems. Below are some things you should consider.

Are you always rushing to get ready for school or work? If so, choose a cut which is quick and easy to style.

Do you play a lot of sport? If so, choose a short style, or one which can easily be tied back.

Do you swim regularly? If so, choose a style which does not rely on blow drying to stay in shape.

Do you study or have a desk job? If so, avoid long bangs that will flop forward on to your face.

Cost

Maintaining a hairstyle can be expensive. Short, geometric hairstyles in particular need frequent visits to the hairdresser to keep them in shape. Dyed hair can look unattractive if the roots are not regularly re-touched and a perm which is growing out can look unkempt. It is therefore important to be realistic about what you can afford to spend after the initial expense of a new hairstyle.

On the right are some points to bear in mind.

★ To keep your style in shape and your hair in good condition, you should have a trim every six weeks.

★ If you have a long, simple style, you may need to have it trimmed only every eight weeks, as long as it is in good condition.

★ A permanent all-over color will need to be re-touched every four weeks as by this time your re-growth will be about 1.3cm long and very noticeable.

★ Permanent highlights or lowlights can be re-touched when you feel it necessary as the re-growth is not as noticeable as that of an all-over color.

★ Re-perming your hair as it starts to grow out can be damaging. However, you will still need to have it trimmed regularly.

★ Bargain haircuts may not be the good value that they seem as you could get a poor style which needs reshaping.

Choosing a hairdresser

Once you have an idea of the kind of hairstyle you would like, you need to find a hairdresser you trust. Start with the salon. If it is within your price range and you like the look of the decor and the staff, you will probably be in tune with the stylist who cuts your hair. Below are some suggestions for things to consider when choosing a salon.

For a first appointment, you are usually booked in with any stylist who has a suitable vacancy. It is a good idea to ask for a consultation first. This gives you a chance to meet them and discuss possible styles. On the opposite page you can find out how to get the most out of a consultation, as well as some tips to bear in mind when you visit the salon.

What to look for in a salon

The outside: you can tell quite a lot about a salon without going inside. Look at the style of the shop front, the name of the salon and the reception area. If they appeal, then there is a good chance that this is the right salon for you. There should also be a price list displayed. Check what things cost and whether you can afford a senior stylist.

The inside: a good salon will be clean, friendly and efficient. The receptionist should be attentive and helpful. Do not be rushed into making an appointment. Ask for a consultation (see right) and have a good look around. If you don't like the look of things, do not be afraid to leave. You are unlikely to get what you want in a salon which makes you feel uncomfortable or intimidated.

Look for modern equipment such as blowdryers, mousses and large combs. Avoid salons that are cluttered with rollers, hairsprays and hooded dryers.

Barbicide jars show that the salon is careful about hygiene.

Photographs on the walls may give you ideas for a new style.

A range of shampoos and conditioners for sale is all part of a good professional service.

Decor should be simple, bright and well-lit.

Shiny basins and well-swept floors are signs of a clean, well kept salon.

Many salons play background music. This can be a good clue to the tastes of the staff.

Schools, training evenings and academies.

These provide an alternative, if you can't afford the prices in a top salon. In a school or at a training session*, your hair is cut and styled by a trainee, under the close supervision of an experienced tutor. Students learn different techniques on different days, so check the timetable before you go along. Provided you go at the right time, you can expect to have nearly as much choice in the style you have as you would get from a qualified stylist.

In an academy, your hair is styled by a qualified hairdresser who is learning advanced techniques. A stylist at this level usually wants to experiment more than a novice. As you are getting expert attention, the stylist will expect to have more influence over your choice of style, than if you were paying the full salon rate.

These are usually held in salons.

Prices

Before booking an appointment check the salon's prices. A price list should be clearly displayed in reception.

★ Find out whether you pay more for a senior stylist. If you only want a trim, choose a junior stylist.

★ Look out for special offers, many salons have discounts on certain days, or concessions for people under 16.

★ See if there are any extras, such as a charge for conditioner.

★ Look out for coupons in magazines advertising discounts.

★ It is worth investigating salons that hand out leaflets in the street advertising special prices.

★ Ask if the salon has a school. Modelling for students can be a cheap way of having a re-style.

Consultations

Any reputable salon will give you a free consultation, if you ask for it. This is a chance to discuss with a stylist what you would like done, without committing yourself to an appointment.

It is good to have a vague idea of a style you would like, such as whether you want it long or short, straight or curly. Keep an open mind, though. Let the stylist feel your hair and assess its natural tendencies. Talk to him about yourself and your lifestyle; tell him what you like about yourself and what you would like to play down. That way you can choose a style which really suits you in the light of expert advice.

Your appointment

When you arrive for your appointment, you will be given a gown to protect your clothes. Then you will be seated in front of a mirror and the stylist will talk to you about what you want done (you may have changed your mind since the consultation).

Next your hair will be shampooed. This takes place in the washing area of the salon and is usually done by a junior. You will then be returned to the cutting chair, where your hair will be cut and styled. If you are having your hair colored or permed, you may have to move to another area of the salon for this stage. The hairdresser will show you the finished style from every angle using a back-mirror (see page 153).

Finally the stylist will brush down your clothes and accompany you back to the reception area to pay your bill.

Dos and don'ts

★ Do ask for any tips and hints on styling your hair, so that you know how to maintain your new style.

★ Do tell the stylist what you really think of the finished style. It is not too late for minor adjustments if you are not completely happy with it.

★ Don't feel obliged to have extras such as conditioner, if you don't feel it is necessary.

★ Don't be afraid to tell the staff what's on your mind. For example, if the water is too hot or cold, when you are being shampooed, or if the stylist is cutting off too much hair.

★ Don't feel you have to leave a tip. If you are pleased with your new style and the service you received, you may want to give the hairdresser something to show your appreciation — it's for you to decide.

How often should you go?

When you have found a hairdresser you like, it is important to go back every six to eight weeks, for a trim. This will keep split ends at bay and your chosen hairstyle looking its best. Ask for your new stylist by name when you book the next appointment.

Hair care routine

Clean, well-groomed hair can make all the difference to the way you feel about yourself. Over time you may have picked up bad habits, such as using too much shampoo or not rinsing your hair adequately. By following the routine outlined on these two pages you will not only notice a marked improvement in your hair's condition but discover that taking extra time over your hair care can be relaxing and fun. All the equipment you need for your new routine is shown on the right.

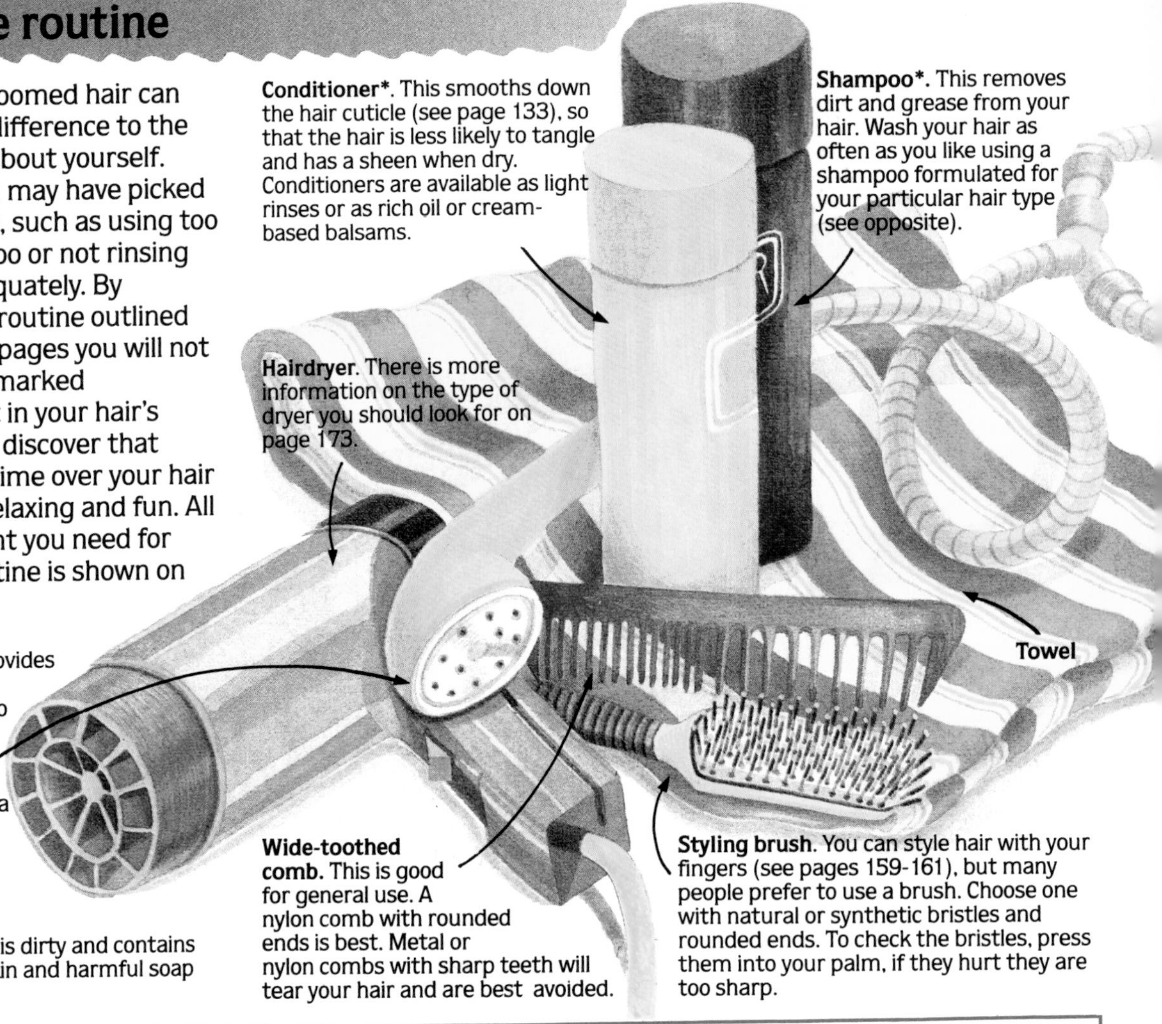

Conditioner*. This smooths down the hair cuticle (see page 133), so that the hair is less likely to tangle and has a sheen when dry. Conditioners are available as light rinses or as rich oil or cream-based balsams.

Shampoo*. This removes dirt and grease from your hair. Wash your hair as often as you like using a shampoo formulated for your particular hair type (see opposite).

Hairdryer. There is more information on the type of dryer you should look for on page 173.

Towel

Shower. This provides constant clean water in which to flush away the dirt and grease in your hair. If you do not have a shower, use running tap water or a cup. Never rinse your hair in bath water as it is dirty and contains bits of flaking skin and harmful soap residue.

Wide-toothed comb. This is good for general use. A nylon comb with rounded ends is best. Metal or nylon combs with sharp teeth will tear your hair and are best avoided.

Styling brush. You can style hair with your fingers (see pages 159-161), but many people prefer to use a brush. Choose one with natural or synthetic bristles and rounded ends. To check the bristles, press them into your palm, if they hurt they are too sharp.

Shampooing and conditioning

Brush your hair to loosen any dirt and dead skin cells. Now wet your hair with luke-warm water. Pour a little shampoo into the palm of your hand. Dilute it slightly with water and rub your palms together to work up a lather.

Massage the shampoo into your hair with your fingertips, starting at your scalp and working right down to the ends. Now rinse it with luke-warm water until the water runs clear. Repeat if your hair is very dirty.

Pat your hair with a towel to soak up most of the moisture.** Gently massage a small amount of conditioner into your hair. Then comb it through, starting with the ends and working back gradually towards the roots.

Leave the conditioner on your hair for the time recommended on the bottle, then rinse it thoroughly in luke-warm water. Finally, rinse it for about 10 seconds in cold water. This will make your hair shinier.

There is more information about the various shampoos and conditioners available on pages 170-171.
** If applied to soaking wet hair, the conditioner will be too dilute.

Blow drying

Pat your hair gently with a towel. Sit in front of a mirror which is close to a power point so that you can move the dryer around freely.

Divide your hair into sections. Dry the lower layers first, clipping the rest out of the way. Dry the back first, then the sides and top. Finish with the front and bangs.

Hold your dryer at least 10cm away from your hair. Put it on to a low setting and move gently back and forth until the section is dry.

As you dry your hair, lift it up. This gives it extra body and speeds up the drying process. Allow the hair to cool before removing the brush.

Brushing and combing

Brushing or combing your hair too often will damage it, so try not to do it more than two or three times a day.

Your hair is particularly vulnerable when it is wet, so always use a wide-toothed comb and treat it gently.

◄ Remove any tangles with a wide-toothed comb. Gently ease them free working through small sections of hair. Start at the ends and move up towards the roots. Hold your hair firmly to avoid pulling on the scalp.

Brush your hair starting at your scalp and moving towards the ends. Then bend forwards and brush the hair down from the nape of your neck. Finally, smooth your hair back in place with your hands. ►

Type	Shampoo	Conditioner	Tips
Greasy	Mild shampoo formulated for greasy hair. These contain little, or no oil.	Light conditioning rinse (avoid oil-based or creamy conditioners). Apply to ends only.	Wash in luke-warm water and brush as little as possible. Use a natural bristle brush (this helps to absorb oil). Between washes, cleanse scalp with an astringent (see page 135).
Dry	Oil-enriched shampoo formulated for dry hair.	Use a cream or balsam conditioner after every wash.	If possible let hair dry naturally and avoid heated appliances. Use a conditioning oil treatment once a week. These can be bought or made at home (see page 134).
Combin-ation	Very mild shampoo.	Oil-based conditioner. Apply to the ends of the hair only.	Use an astringent between washes (see page 135). Choose a style which can be left to dry naturally, rather than using heated appliances.
Normal	Mild shampoo.	Light conditioning rinse (not a cream conditioner) after every wash.	At the first sign of damage, treat with a single conditioning oil treatment (see page 134).

Special effects

Whether your hair is long or short, it is still possible to give it a totally different look and texture — be it for a party, on vacation or just for a change. The styling products and accessories shown here will give you some ideas. On page 172 you can find out about each individual product in more detail.

Mousse

Mousse adds body and texture to all hair types and is especially effective on styles that are scrunch dried (see page 159). You can buy regular or firm hold. Apply it to the roots of damp hair with your fingertips, then smooth it evenly through your hair with the palms of your hands.

Gel

Gel can be used to make shorter styles look spiky, or to keep a style in place to add body. Wet-look gel has a glossy finish. Apply gel to the roots of towel-dried or dry hair with your fingertips and then smooth it through with the palms of your hands.

Glaze

Glaze is stronger than gel and sets hard on your hair. It is particularly effective for slicking back curly or layered hair. Smooth it through towel-dried hair with the palms of your hands. Do not apply it to the roots of your hair.

Creams and greases

Creams and greases can give hair a healthy sheen or create a slicked-back wet look depending on how much you apply. Smooth it through wet or dry hair with the palms of your hands.

Finishing spray

Finishing spray coats the finished style in a fine mist of oil so that it looks healthy and shiny. It is especially effective on sleek, one-length styles and slicked-back hair. It can also be used to highlight different colors in hair.

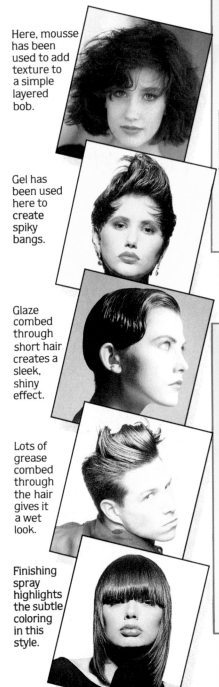

Here, mousse has been used to add texture to a simple layered bob.

Gel has been used here to create spiky bangs.

Glaze combed through short hair creates a sleek, shiny effect.

Lots of grease combed through the hair gives it a wet look.

Finishing spray highlights the subtle coloring in this style.

Accessories

Accessories such as ribbons, slides and combs are useful for keeping hair out of your way. They can also add variety to your hairstyle and allow you to color co-ordinate your clothes and hair.

When looking for new accessories, make sure that items such as slides and combs are strong enough to hold your hair in place and that they do not have sharp teeth or edges which might tear it. Choose colors which complement your clothes and stand out well against your hair color.

For a special occasion, colored chopsticks pushed through a top-knot give an oriental look.

Instant color

If you want a quick change of color for a party or a disco, try an instant spray-on hair color. This is a type of lacquer which coats the hair shaft with color. Sprays are available in a variety of vivid color and some even contain glitter or produce a metallic sheen on your hair. Instant colorants can either be washed or brushed out of your hair.

Here the hair has been sprayed several different colors.

Hair extensions

Hair extensions are made of fine strands of nylon which are melted around your natural hair. They are available in almost any color, texture or length. Hair extensions must be attached by a professional hairdresser. It is difficult and risky to attempt it yourself. Extensions last for up to four months (after this, the bond will begin to loosen) and are washed in the same way as normal hair. You can remove them by twisting the braid and gently snapping the seal.

The hair extension is placed on the parting of a small tress and the hair criss-crossed over the extension.

The real hair and the hair extension are then tightly plaited together and painted with a bonding solution.

A heated clamp melts the solution, sealing the extension around the hair. This is known as heat sealing.

Here, an intricate pattern has been painted onto the hair extensions.

Wigs and hair pieces

Synthetic wigs and hair pieces can be fun to wear and need not be too expensive. Some look and feel like real hair (these are the most expensive kind), others are brightly colored and are meant to look false (these can be bought very cheaply). Either type quickly and easily transforms your looks and needs minimal care. Before putting on a wig, pin your own hair into flat curls. Pull on the wig from the front holding it firmly at your forehead.

Hair pieces can either be plaited into your hair or attached with grips.

Disguise unkempt hair which is in poor condition with a wig.

Use hair pieces to add body or length.

Wigs and hair pieces should be brushed and shampooed regularly. Clean them in cool water and leave them to drip-dry. They automatically revert to their original shape when they are dry.

To store wigs and hair pieces, wrap them in tissue paper and put in a box in a cool place. Alternatively, wigs can be turned inside out and hung on a doorknob or on a special wig block.

Braiding

Braiding is a traditional technique used to style Afro hair. The hair is divided into lots of tiny little plaits which can be decorated with ribbons or beads and arranged in various styles.

Braided hair can be left in place for up to two months*. To keep it clean use a hand shower and direct the water along the partings so that the shampoo washes through the hair. Rosemary or almond oil, rubbed gently into your scalp, will help keep it healthy.

Braiding. Divide long hair into small square sections and braid them tightly. Seal the ends with wax or tie them with cotton.

Cornrowing. Part short hair into long thin rows. Braid each row tightly against the head, weaving wisps of hair into the braid to give a neat finish.

Wrapping. Wind special cotton thread tightly around sections of hair. You can then arrange the strands into intricate patterns on the head.

Do not braid or wrap your hair for longer than this. It strains the scalp and can cause hair loss.

Nostalgic hairstyles

This century, variety in women's hairstyles has increased enormously. This is because of changing attitudes (which have made short hair acceptable for women) and the development of new styling techniques, such as perming.

Innovations in men's hairdressing have been slower to develop. However, since the 1950s, men have also enjoyed a wider choice of styles.

Here you can see the hairstyles for which each decade, from the 1920s to the 1980s, is best remembered.

1920s

In the 1920s, women began to wear their hair short for the first time. This complemented a fashion for simple, uninhibiting clothes and shorter skirts. A silent film star called Louise Brooks popularised the bob (see page 154).

Men's hairstyles of the 1920s were short and smart. Oil was often used to slick the hair back and make it glossy.

Louise Brooks popularised the bob.

Rudolph Valentino, a famous screen idol, wore a typical 1920s hair style.

1950s

Men's and women's hairstyles changed dramatically in the 1950s.

Young men started to evolve distinctive styles of their own, based on teen idols such as Elvis Presley, James Dean and Buddy Holly. Hair was worn much longer (sometimes collar-length). It was slicked back, as before, but often with a huge, exaggerated quiff at the front.

Elvis Presley's hairstyle was his trademark.

Audrey Hepburn in the film 'Breakfast at Tiffany's'

It was still fashionable for women to wear their hair up. Teenage girls wore pony tails. Older women favoured back-combing which involved combing the hair upwards, then teasing it back towards the roots to give body. The hair could then be piled high on the head and sculpted into outlandish shapes. The finished style would be kept in place using hairspray.

1970s

In the early 70s, the graduated cut (see pages 156-157) and the shaggy perm made hair care easier than ever before as both looks required minimal styling. The feather cut was popular with men and women alike. It was short on top, with long, wispy strands of hair framing the face. Rock star David Bowie and film star Jane Fonda both wore versions of the feather cut.

Casual, wash and wear styles were a feature of the 1970s.

This Mohican hairstyle was popular with 70s punks.

In the mid 70s, punk rock music inspired a new fashion cult in which hair played a large part.

Punks rejected conventional fashion, wearing clothes which were often deliberately ripped or defaced with graffiti. They dyed their hair bright colors, such as green or orange, and used sprays or gels to sculpt it into threatening spiky styles.

1930s

In the 1930s, film stars such as Jean Harlow inspired women to dye their hair and wear it longer.

1940s

Long hair continued to be popular for women in the 1940s. Now however, it was more often worn up or tied back, with rolls or waves to give fullness at the front. A new and better perming method made curly hair more popular than ever.

The only difference between men's hairstyles of the 1940s and those of the 1920s was that side partings became the fashion.

Joan Crawford wearing a typical 1940s hair style.

Clark Gable. Men's hair cuts had not changed much since the 1920s.

1960s

The 60s was a time of great variety. Informal looks which were easy to care for matched the relaxed attitudes of the decade. Vidal Sassoon revived the bob, but gave it a distinctive modern look by using revolutionary cutting and blow drying techniques. This made it an emblem of the times.

During the late 60s, long hair was fashionable for both sexes.

The 1960s version of the bob.

Afro styles or long hair characterized the hippy look.

The Beatles influenced men's hair styles.

1980s

The casual, sporty hairstyles of the early 80s gave way, by the middle of the decade, to several more stylised looks. These often featured short, rounded bangs and geometric lines. Although they appeared very formal, such styles did not actually require much attention to keep in shape. The 20s-style crop made a come-back in the 80s (this time dyed blonde).

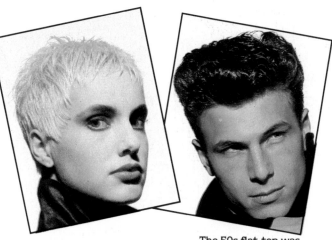

A bleached crop

The 50s flat-top was revived for men.

Men's hairstyles got shorter and shorter until the late 80s. Towards the middle of the decade, there was a trend for cropped styles with a small plait at the nape. Later, a flat-top style, reminiscent of the 1950s took over from this. Long hair for men was also revived, but the 80s version was sleek and well-groomed, unlike the unkempt styles of the 60s.

Becoming a hairdresser

Hairdressing is a popular and exciting career which requires a wide variety of skills and personal attributes, from physical fitness to artistic judgement. Hairdressing training is undergoing important changes which will result in more possibilities for travel and variety of work than ever before, as the skills needed to do the job become standardized internationally. Here you can find out about the personal qualities you need to enter the profession, your promotion prospects and where hairdressing might lead you.

What does it take to be a hairdresser?

Below you can find out what kind of person makes a good hairdresser. It is worth considering not only whether you are right for the job, but also whether it is right for you.

Don't be put off if you are weak in some areas; many of the skills come with training. The first requirement is enthusiasm and an awareness of what hairdressing involves.

Physical qualities

Hairdressers are on their feet most of the day, and some of the styling techniques are demanding physically, so you will need to be fit.

Trainees keep the salon clean and tidy. This can be tiring.

Do not go into hairdressing if you suffer from skin disorders, such as eczema. Constantly getting your hands wet and handling strong chemicals may make your condition worse.

Some hairdressing techniques require good co-ordination.

Most of the tasks involved in cutting hair require manual dexterity (the ability to handle tools efficiently). This comes with practice, but it helps if you have good co-ordination.

Personal attributes

You will need to be patient and reasonably outgoing. Learning to communicate well and deal with people sympathetically comes with practice. It helps if you are naturally a sociable person and have an easy-going temperament.

A client who is disappointed with her new hairstyle needs to be treated with tact.

As well as requiring technical skills, hairdressing is also a creative and artistic job. If you are attracted by it, then you probably have some interest in fashion and beauty. Try to cultivate this and develop an eye for color and a sense of shape, symmetry and proportion.

Qualifications

You need a good basic education to be a hairdresser. You should be literate (able to read and write well) and numerate (able to do basic math). These skills are particularly important if your ambition is to become a salon manager. A manager needs to be able to communicate well (verbally and on paper) and to understand basic accounting and stock control methods.

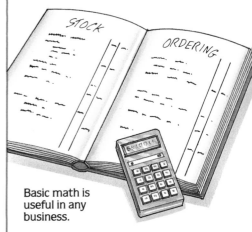

Basic math is useful in any business.

Any further qualifications you may have need not be wasted in hairdressing. For example, languages are useful if you want to work abroad (see opposite) and history could help you to get a job in film or television (see page 169).

Training as a hairdresser

Training schemes vary in format and length from country to country:

UK and Europe*

Training is currently being standardized so that each country's requirements of a newly qualified hairdresser are the same. This means that hairdressers will be able to move freely between countries and their skills will be recognized throughout the continent. On page 175 you can find out where to write for further information on training in the UK.

USA

In the USA you are expected to have a basic qualification in cosmetology (the science of skin and hair) before you can train as a hairdresser. On page 175, there is an address you can write to for details of hairdressing courses in the USA.

Advanced training

Once you are working as a hairdresser more advanced training is available which will give you the additional skills you need to climb the promotional ladder (see right). You may also have the opportunity to specialize in a particular area, or to learn management skills.

Competitions

Qualified hairdressers sometimes enter competitions. These can be run by companies which manufacture hairdressing products or alternatively, organized between several salons in one chain.

Competitions help to keep stylists in touch with new developments and provide them with an opportunity to experiment creatively.
Winning a competition can help a stylist's reputation and employment prospects.
Salons benefit from the publicity which competitions attract.

Promotion prospects

The ladder on the right represents the promotion route which exists in most salons. Once qualified, a hairdresser can decide whether to stay in the salon and progress up the ladder (following the blue arrows) or whether to move sideways, into a different area of the industry (following the pink arrows).

Specialize in one area and become advisor to large organization.

Teach in a hairdressing school.

Become a ship's hairdresser or work abroad.

Move into films, theatre or television.

School or other career

Salon manager. May be senior stylist. Recruits and supervises staff. Handles staff problems. Deals with salon finance, public relations and publicity. Sometimes acts as creative director, developing the salon's image and 'market profile'.

Senior stylist. Cuts, barbers, perms and colors hair to a very high professional standard. Develops creative talents. May start to specialize in one area, such as coloring or perming.

Stylist. Cuts, barbers, perms and colors hair to a high professional standard. May do advanced hairdressing courses and enter competitions.

Junior stylist (or first year operator). Cuts, barbers, perms and colors hair to a professional standard without supervision.

Trainee. Shampoos hair. Does roller setting, pin curling, finger waving. Learns science of skin and hair and salon etiquette. Learns basic cutting, barbering, coloring and perming. Cleans salon. Helps stylists.

Become an executive in a large hairdressing company or manage own chain of salons.

Work for the fashion and advertising businesses (styling hair for catwalk shows or photography sessions) as well as in a salon.

Demonstrate hairstyling products (see pages 172-173).

Equipment

As a trainee hairdresser, you will be learning the practice as well as the theory of hairdressing.

On these two pages you can find out about all the equipment you will be using.

Hairdresser's own equipment

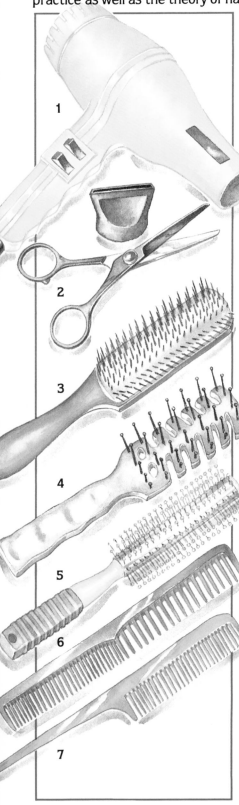

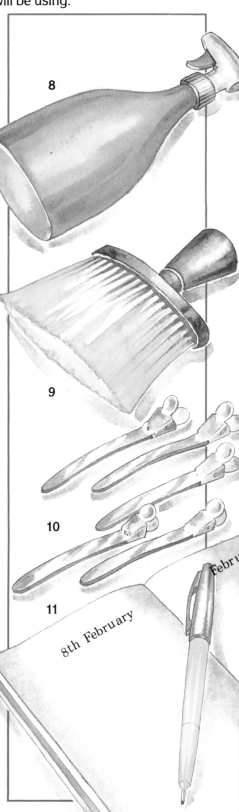

1. Hairdryer. Choose a lightweight, powerful dryer with several different temperature settings.

2. Scissors. These are a hairdresser's most important tool and it is well worth spending the money to buy a really good pair. Your employer or course tutor should be able to advise you on where to buy them from. Look for a pair with short blades (about 10-11cm long) as these will give you maximum control. Have your scissors sharpened regularly, as blunt blades create an uneven cutting line.

3. Styling brush. For general styling, choose a brush with rounded nylon bristles set into a flexible rubber pad. This type of brush is very hygienic, as it can be taken apart for cleaning.

4. Vent brush. When styling curly hair, you will need a brush with rounded nylon bristles, set into a flat, vented base.

5. Radial brush. Good for blow-drying hair in a curly style.

6. Wide-toothed comb. Choose a comb made of plastic or hardened rubber. The teeth should have rounded ends.

7. Tail comb. Useful for separating tresses when coloring or curling hair (using the tail). The teeth should have rounded ends and should be made of plastic or hardened rubber. The tail may be metal.

8. Spray mist. Useful for dampening sections of hair which may have started to dry during cutting.

9. Neckbrush. For removing tiny strands of hair from your client's neck and face.

10. Sectioning clips. For clipping hair out of your way while you work on a particular section.

11. Appointments diary. For writing down your own daily schedule.

Salon equipment

All salons have the following basic equipment:

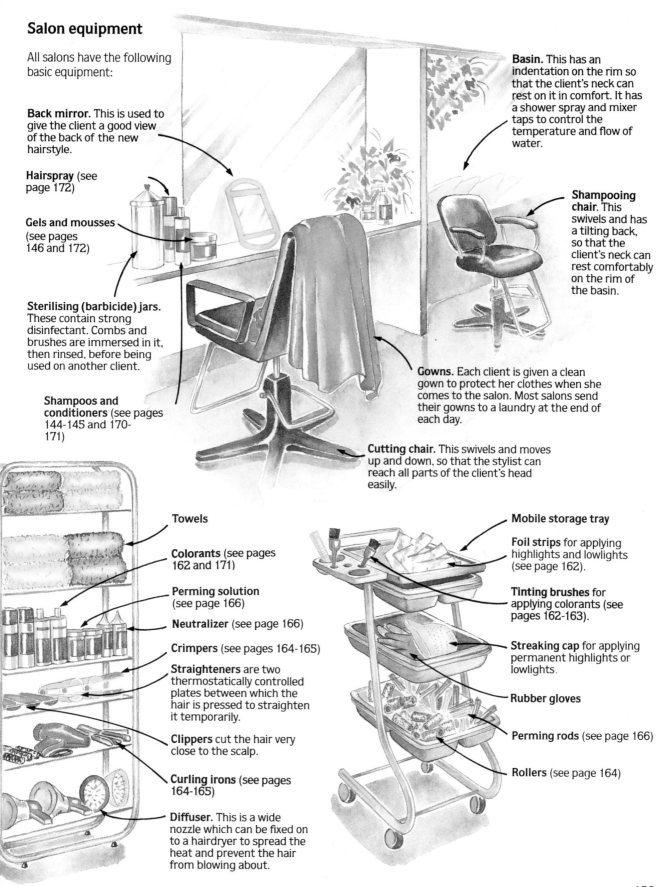

Back mirror. This is used to give the client a good view of the back of the new hairstyle.

Hairspray (see page 172)

Gels and mousses (see pages 146 and 172)

Sterilising (barbicide) jars. These contain strong disinfectant. Combs and brushes are immersed in it, then rinsed, before being used on another client.

Shampoos and conditioners (see pages 144-145 and 170-171)

Basin. This has an indentation on the rim so that the client's neck can rest on it in comfort. It has a shower spray and mixer taps to control the temperature and flow of water.

Shampooing chair. This swivels and has a tilting back, so that the client's neck can rest comfortably on the rim of the basin.

Gowns. Each client is given a clean gown to protect her clothes when she comes to the salon. Most salons send their gowns to a laundry at the end of each day.

Cutting chair. This swivels and moves up and down, so that the stylist can reach all parts of the client's head easily.

Towels

Colorants (see pages 162 and 171)

Perming solution (see page 166)

Neutralizer (see page 166)

Crimpers (see pages 164-165)

Straighteners are two thermostatically controlled plates between which the hair is pressed to straighten it temporarily.

Clippers cut the hair very close to the scalp.

Curling irons (see pages 164-165)

Diffuser. This is a wide nozzle which can be fixed on to a hairdryer to spread the heat and prevent the hair from blowing about.

Mobile storage tray

Foil strips for applying highlights and lowlights (see page 162).

Tinting brushes for applying colorants (see pages 162-163).

Streaking cap for applying permanent highlights or lowlights.

Rubber gloves

Perming rods (see page 166)

Rollers (see page 164)

Professional cutting methods

Despite the apparent abundance of highly individual styles, they all evolved from one of three basic cuts – the bob, the graduated cut or the layered look.

Over the next eight pages you can find out how the professionals are taught these basic cuts and how, with the aid of new techniques and versatile styling products, the looks can be adapted to create a wider variety of styles than ever before.

All the cutting techniques illustrated here should be carried out under the supervision of a qualified instructor.

The rules of cutting

The secret of successful hairstyling is understanding your client's hair. Below are some basic rules. You can find out about the equipment you will need on pages 152-153.

1. Always cut hair wet, because:

★ Freshly washed hair is more hygienic to work with.
★ The hair is easier to control.
★ The client's head shape is clearly visible and the shape of the cut is more easily defined.
★ Washing the hair removes substances such as mousse or gel which affects the way it falls.

2. Use the natural shape of the head as a guideline when cutting.

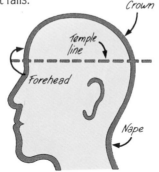

Here you can see the names given to the different parts of the head. These terms are used in the step-by-step cutting instructions which follow.

3. Consider the natural growth of the hair.

Hair grows from a natural base on the crown. This should dictate the way in which it is cut as working against the natural growth will result in a bad style. Hair also has a natural parting and hairline. A style which attempts to create an artificial line will look odd and may be hard to manage.

4. Hold the hair firmly but without tension.

Pulling hair tightly distorts the cutting line. The hair will spring back to its natural position once it is released, creating an uneven line.

5. Compensate for the ears

When cutting a style which covers the ears, compensate for the fact that they will make the hair lift slightly.

The bob

In the early 1920s, the silent filmstar, Louise Brooks, created a sensation by wearing her hair in a stark, chic style which became known as the bob. The look was revived amid great publicity in the 1960s, when Vidal Sassoon styled a bangless version for the actress Nancy Kwan. Since then, the bob has been consistently popular in one form or another.

The bob is a one-length hairstyle. This means that if an imaginary line is drawn horizontally around the bottom of the hair, all the ends touch it. A banged bob is just a variation on the same theme. All one-length styles, whether long or short, are based on this cut.

Probably the most versatile of the basic cuts, the bob can be adapted to suit almost any hair type and face shape. The sleek, sculptured look is ideal for heavy, straight hair, while wavy hair will produce a softer style and curly hair a really dramatic effect.

Adapting the basic cut

This subtle wavy effect has been achieved by cutting the bob short at the back and then gradually lengthening it towards the front of the head. A soft pin curl perm* has then been applied, and the hair left to dry naturally. ▶

Cutting*

1. Part the hair at the back and clip one side out of the way. On the free side, comb the bottom layer of hair on to the neck as shown. Cut the layer to length (this is known as 'cutting in the base line').

2. Comb down another layer of hair and hold it firmly in place at the nape. Using the base line as a guide, cut it the same length as before. Repeat this procedure until the back section is completed.

3. Move around to the side of the head. Hold the bottom layer of hair away from the neck as shown. This compensates for the ear. Cut the hair so that it lines up with the base line at the back of the head.

4. Working up towards the top of the head, gradually release fine layers of hair and cut each one to the length of the base line. Now repeat steps three and four on the other half of the head.

Drying

5. Finally, cut the bangs as follows. First comb out the hair and flatten it against the forehead with one hand. Then, holding the scissors in the other hand, cut the bangs to the required length.

6. Now hold the centre section of the bangs slightly away from the forehead, as shown. Cut it in a straight line. This creates a layered effect and gives the finished bangs a softer look.

1. Divide the hair into sections as for cutting. Hold the dryer about 10cm from the hair. Brush from underneath, directing the heat on to the brush as it moves from the roots to the ends of the hair.

2. Always point the hairdryer down towards the ends of the hair as you dry. Keep each section quite fine, and make sure that it is completely dry before moving on to the next one.

◄ These sides were cut by sliding the scissors along each tress**. This produces a mixture of lengths and reduces weight. It is known as 'slide cutting'.

The bangs have been cut ► a little further back than the temples, and curved slightly. When the hair is worn up, there is still a strong line around the face.

Here, the hair has been cut in a heavy square line. The front section was then twisted and slide cut (see left) to give an ◄ impression of ringlets.

Remember, only cut hair under the supervision of a qualified instructor.
**A small section or lock of hair.*

The graduated cut

The graduated look combines a bold outline with a softer feathery effect. This look first became popular in the 1970s and is the basis for many of today's softer, shorter styles.

It is generally used to add body and movement to straight hair, but can also be successfully adapted to most hair types. The graduated cut suits most face shapes, although it is not recommended if you have a very heavy or wide jaw-line.

The most popular haircuts for men are based on the short graduated cut (as shown on the left) and the short layered cut (shown on pages 158-159). Long hair for men has been in fashion from time to time, particularly in the late 60s when the hippy look was popular.

Cutting*

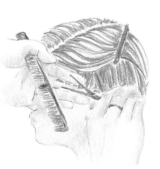

1. First comb the hair and let it fall into its natural parting. Now, taking this into account, cut the basic outline shape. This is called the base line, and dictates the length of the cut.

2. Comb down the bottom layer of hair on one side and clip the rest out of your way. To create a soft line, hold the hair away from the head and cut to the required length.

4. When you reach the layers of hair closest to the temple line, hold them downwards, much closer to the head as shown. This helps to create a much stronger line.

5. When you reach the final layer of hair, hold the hair out horizontally from the head and cut to length. This gives an even, rounded shape to the finished cut.

Drying

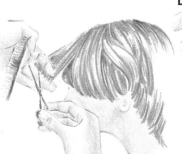
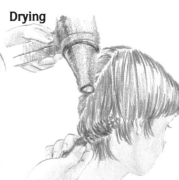

7. Cut the bangs last as it is easier to judge the final length when almost dry. Hold the bangs slightly forward and cut on a curve to create a heavy rounded effect.

1. To dry the hair, divide it into sections in the same way as you did for cutting. Using a styling brush and hairdryer, follow the same technique as for drying the bob (see page 155).

*Remember, only cut hair under the supervision of a qualified instructor.

3. Separate the next layer of hair and cut it so that it falls just below the first one. Continue in this way until you reach the layer of hair which is nearest to the temple line.

6. Repeat this method on the other side. When you have completed both sides, graduate the back in the same way, to reduce the hair between the nape and crown.

2. If you want the finished look to be soft and feathery, use the brush to turn the hair outwards, rather than inwards. This gives a slight curve to the top sections of hair.

Adapting the basic cut

It is easy to transform the basic graduated cut into a glamorous look for evenings.

Here, mousse was applied to the roots, then the hair was directed upwards and backwards while being finger dried (see page 161).

You can find out more about mousse and other styling products on page 172.

To achieve the effect shown here, naturally curly or wavy hair has been left to dry by itself.

Straight hair would need to be softly permed after it has been cut in a graduated style. The hair would then be left to dry naturally.

This naturally curly graduated cut has been made more dramatic by clipping the hair very short at the back and sides.

First, the basic style was cut. Then clippers (see page 153) were used to cut the hair very close to the head. This technique is known as 'cropping'.

Here, a deep base line has been cut to create a fuller, heavier graduated style. This is known as a 'rounded graduation'

The lower layers have been tinted a darker shade than the rest of the hair to give them added depth. The hair has then been styled using a generous amount of mousse to give it extra body.

To produce the spiky effect shown here, scissors have been woven in and out of small sections of hair so that some sections are cut shorter than others. The shorter sections have been spaced as evenly as possible.

This technique is known as 'weave cutting'. The finished effect is one of added height and body.

Layering short hair

The basic layered cut can be worn short or long, and for this reason, it is probably the most popular look in modern hairdressing.

Originally regarded as a cut for men, the short layered look was adopted by women in the early 1920s.

Shorter hairstyles and less restrictive clothing were popular at this time because women had worked outside the home during the First World War and this led to a new mood of emancipation and practicality afterwards. One of the most extreme cuts to emerge was the Eton crop (named after the famous English boy's school) for which the hair was cut very short around the ears.

The short layered cut is a style that is suited to all hair types and can be adapted to flatter almost all the basic face shapes.

Cutting*

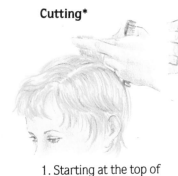

1. Starting at the top of the head, separate a section of hair from the crown, as shown. Comb the rest of the hair out of the way and clip if necessary.

2. Hold the hair horizontally, and pull it forward towards the front of the head. Cut the hair straight across. Repeat with each layer until you reach the bang area.

3. To check that you have cut the hair evenly, hold it lengthways, as shown. Trim off any uneven ends leaving the hair slightly longer near the crown.** This is 'cross-checking'.

4. Cut the back section starting at the crown and working down towards the nape. Take a layer of hair from the back of the crown and hold it vertically, as shown.

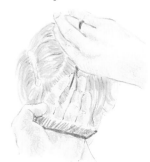

5. Pull the hair slightly away from the head and cut it with the scissors pointing towards the nape of the neck, rather than across the head. Repeat until all the hair is cut.

6. Now check that the back section is the correct length by holding the hair horizontally as shown, and trimming away any of the ends which are not aligned (cross-checking).

7. Cut the sides from the crown downwards in the same way as the back. Check that the layers are even by running the fingers up through the hair. Trim any uneven ends.

8. To cut the bangs, hold them out slightly from the forehead and cut so they fall in a soft line. Finally, trim the base line to the required length. This gives the cut its shape.

*Remember, only cut hair under the supervision of a qualified instructor.
** If the hair is too short near the crown it will stick up when dry.

Drying

The best way to style short layered hair is by running your fingers through it, or scrunching it (see right) until it dries. These techniques give the hair an attractive tousled look. Allowing hair to dry naturally is better for it. However, this is not always possible in the salon. You can speed up the technique shown here and still achieve a similar result by using a hairdryer on a low setting.

Finger drying: first towel dry the hair, leaving it slightly damp. Then massage through a generous amount of mousse (see page 172) to keep the style in place. Keeping your fingers straight, run each hand alternately through the hair, at the same time lifting it up from the roots to add body and movement to the finished style. ▶

Scrunch drying: Towel dry the hair until it is only slightly damp and add plenty of mousse. Arrange roughly the style you want. Then take handfuls of hair and scrunch them gently in your fist, using the palm of your hand to push the hair up from the scalp. As you scrunch the hair, gently massage it with your fingers to remove all the moisture. ◀

Adapting the basic cut

Here, the hair has been 'twist cut' in order to achieve a full, bouncy texture. This technique involves taking small sections of the hair and twisting them, before cutting. ▶

Color can then be added to make the look even more dramatic, as here.

To create this stunning effect, the hair has been cut in very short layers, then gel applied to the roots. The hair was then finger dried (see above). Finally, the tips of the hair were tinted a slightly darker color (there is more about coloring hair on pages 162-163). ▶

To produce soft, wispy bangs, small sections of hair have been cut every few millimetres, with the scissors pointing down towards the ends of the hair. This cutting technique is known as 'pointing'. ▶

To give a cut this unusual elongated shape, the hair has been left much longer at the crown than normal. This creates fullness. The short sides and back add to the impression of height. Gel has then been used to keep the hair in place. ▶

For this look, the layers on the top of the head have been left fairly long, and the back and sides cropped very short. This gives an impression of fullness which is complemented by the solid, rounded bangs. ▶

Here, a soft pin curl perm** has been applied to give variety of texture to a straight layered cut. This creates a very subtle soft wave through the top layer of hair. In addition, the model's bangs have been 'pointed' (see left). ▶

You can find out more about applying gel on page 146.
**There is information on perming on pages 166-167.*

Layering long hair

The long layered cut became popular in the early 1970s. It provided a whole new range of styles for people who preferred to wear their hair longer, and a softer alternative to the more severe short layered cut.

Long layered cuts have remained extremely popular in the 1980s as they flatter most face shapes, are easy to maintain and suit almost all hair types. The only things which restrict people from choosing them is having brittle hair or hair with a short life-span (see pages 132-133). Layering longer hair gives it extra body, while making it easier to style and quicker to dry.

The cutting technique used is similar to that for short hair (see pages 158-159), however the layers are left much longer and the cutting stages are reversed so that the basic outline is cut before layering begins, rather than afterwards.

Cutting*

1. Starting with the bangs, hold the hair out at a slight angle from the head, as shown. Carefully cut the hair to the required length, little by little.

2. Move around to the side. Again holding the hair out at a slight angle, cut it to length. This creates a soft outline when the hair dries. Repeat on the other side.

3. Hold the hair at the back of the head against the neck or back** of the client and cut it to length. This establishes the outline (base line) of the cut.

4. To layer the hair, start with the area in front of the crown. Comb out a section of hair and hold it forwards. Cut the hair straight across.

5. Continue in the same way until all the hair in front of the crown is layered. Then move to the sides and layer them as you did the front section.

6. When you reach the crown, hold each layer of hair straight out to the side. This reduces the weight of the top layers. Cut as before.

7. Move around to the back of the head and layer the hair between the nape of the neck and the crown, using the the same method as described in stage 6.

8. Finally, check that the base line is even and cross-check the layers (see page 158) to make sure that there are no untidy ends visible.

* Remember, only cut hair under the supervision of a qualified instructor.
** This depends on the finished length required by the client.

Drying

The long layered cut should ideally be left to dry naturally. This gives it a natural look and is better for the hair. However, in a salon there will not be time to do this. The following steps show you how to achieve a similar effect using gel and a hairdryer.

When drying a client's hair, try to explain what you are doing so that they feel confident about styling their new cut at home.

Towel dry the hair, leaving it slightly damp. Then apply a generous amount of gel (see page 18) to the roots with your fingertips.

Blow dry the roots by lifting the hair with your fingers and directing the heat down into the hair (from at least 10cm away).

If possible, leave the ends of the hair to dry naturally as this will give it added body. It also creates an attractive tousled effect.

Adapting the basic cut

Here you can see how wet-look gel can be effective on long hair. Gel has been combed through the hair, which has then been formed into waves with the fingers. A few strands of hair have been loosened to ► soften the look.

This effect has been achieved on naturally curly hair by cutting the top layers short and leaving the sides and back layers longer. The hair has then been scrunch dried (see page 31). If the hair were straight, it would need to be permed on large rollers first. ►

Here, long, straight hair has been permed on rollers of different sizes to give it a variety of textures. It has then been left to dry naturally. To achieve a soft, romantic effect, the hair around the temples has then been swept away from the ► face and piled loosely on top of the head.

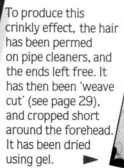

Here, the bangs have been 'pointed' (see page 31) to give a wispy look. To emphasize the layers, the hair has been highlighted with two complementary colors. It has then been finger dried. ►

To produce this crinkly effect, the hair has been permed on pipe cleaners, and the ends left free. It has then been 'weave cut' (see page 29), and cropped short around the forehead. It has been dried using gel. ►

The basic long layered cut works well on naturally wavy hair. To emphasize the soft, feathery effect of the cut, subtle highlights have been added around the face. The hair has then been ► dried using the technique described at the top of the page.

Professional coloring methods

A change of hair color can give new life to a style you are bored with, and trying out different effects can be fun. However, hair colorants are potentially damaging, so it is advisable to have them applied by a professional hairdresser. If you do want to color your hair at home, use a colorant that does not alter your hair chemically (see below) and check with your hairdresser first.

Tools of the trade

Below are some of the tools used for coloring hair.

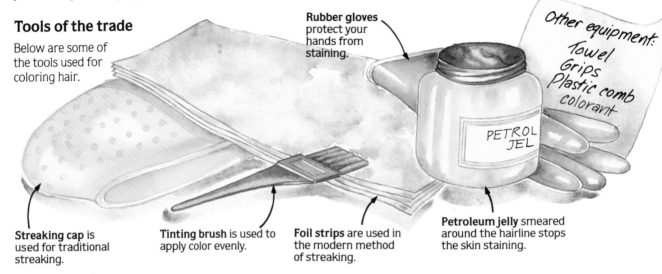

Rubber gloves protect your hands from staining.

Other equipment:
Towel
Grips
Plastic comb
colorant

PETROL JEL

Streaking cap is used for traditional streaking.

Tinting brush is used to apply color evenly.

Foil strips are used in the modern method of streaking.

Petroleum jelly smeared around the hairline stops the skin staining.

Types of colorant

Colorants work by staining the hair shaft with color. The length of time a color lasts depends on how far it penetrates the hair shaft.

Temporary colorants coat the hair shaft with a thin layer of color which is removed by shampooing.* Apply them to damp hair in the form of a liquid or mousse, or on to styled hair if you are using gel, spray or paints.

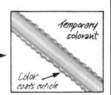

temporary colorant

Color coats cuticle

Semi-permanent colorants last longer than temporary colorants because they enter the cuticle. Apply them to clean hair in the form of a creamy shampoo or mousse.

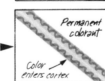

Semi-permanent colorant

Color enters cuticle

Permanent colorants (dyes) or bleaches (see page 171) penetrate deep into the cortex. When mixed with a chemical called hydrogen peroxide they actually change the pigment in the hair (see page 132). Apply them to dry hair

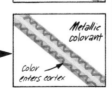

Permanent colorant

Color enters cortex

Metallic colorants are used on greying hair and are known as progressive dyes as the color develops after several applications. They contain lead or silver salts which slowly change color. Apply as a liquid on to dry hair.

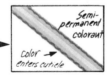

Metallic colorant

Color enters cortex

Vegetable colorants are available in two types. One type coats the cuticle and is applied as an infusion (see page 135). The other, henna for example, penetrates the cortex. Natural dyes fade, so must be applied regularly to maintain the color.

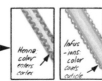

Henna: color enters cortex

Infus-ions: color coats cuticle

Testing colorants

The following tests should be done before coloring your hair, whether at a hairdresser's, or at home.

Strand test: to check that a color suits you, dip a few strands of your hair in the colorant. Leave for the recommended time and rinse clean.

Skin test: Dab a little colorant on the inside of your elbow. Leave for a few hours. If your arm itches or turns red, do not use the product.

Dos and don'ts when coloring at home

★ Do follow the manufacturer's instructions carefully.

★ Do a skin and strand test first.

★ Don't choose a red tint if you have a flushed or ruddy complexion.

★ Don't try bleaching naturally red hair as it will turn a brassy yellow.

★ Don't choose a dark shade if you have a fair complexion.

* You may find that there are still traces of color after one wash.

Applying color

Below you can find out about two of the most popular methods of coloring.

Overall color

1. Divide the hair into quarters by creating two partings: one from the forehead to the nape of the neck and one across the centre of the head.

2. Apply the color to the ends of the hair and leave for 15 minutes. Then apply to the roots and leave for a further 15 minutes.

3. Rinse thoroughly. Shampoo and condition the hair and then style it as normal. The finished effect should be even color.

Foil highlights or lowlights*

1. Separate a section of hair. With a tail comb (see page 152) weave in and out of the section picking up fine tresses of hair.

2. Place the foil under the tresses and use a tinting brush to paint on the colorant.

3. Fold the foil around the hair. Repeat with each section. Leave for the recommended time.

4. Remove the foil strips starting with the first section you did. Rinse thoroughly. Shampoo and condition as normal.

Alternative techniques

Batiking. Lighten the hair and apply petroleum jelly to the areas where no further color is wanted. Paint the exposed areas in three complementary colors. Now comb the hair lightly to blend the colors. The result is a subtle mixture of random colors.

Streaks. Dry hair is combed ▶ into its usual style, then a streaking cap pulled tightly on top. Small strands of hair are then pulled through the holes with a hook, and color applied to them. Once the color has taken effect, the cap is removed, and the hair is rinsed and shampooed thoroughly.

Slices. The hair is combed ▶ into its usual style, then separated into tresses. Each tress is then divided (or sliced) in half widthways, and color is applied to the half nearest the scalp. When the color has taken effect, the hair is rinsed thoroughly.

Flying colors. Color ▶ is applied to the tips of the hair with a brush and comb, then it is left for the recommended time. It is then rinsed, shampooed and styled as usual.

Applying henna

Henna is a natural dye which comes in powdered form. It colors and conditions your hair.

1. Mix the henna with warm water until it looks like mud. Comb it through clean, dry hair.

2. Wrap your hair in plastic wrap or an old towel. Then leave for up to an hour.**

3. Rinse out the henna, until the water runs clear. Finally, shampoo and style your hair as usual.

* Highlights are lighter than your natural color and lowlights darker.
** Check the packet for guidelines on how long to leave the henna.

Professional curling methods

The methods of curling shown here are all used by professional hairdressers. Unlike the cutting techniques shown on pages 154-161, curling can be done successfully at home. The right equipment helps (a selection of tools is shown below), and following the correct procedure is essential. With practice, you should be able to produce various looks – from corkscrew curls to soft waves.

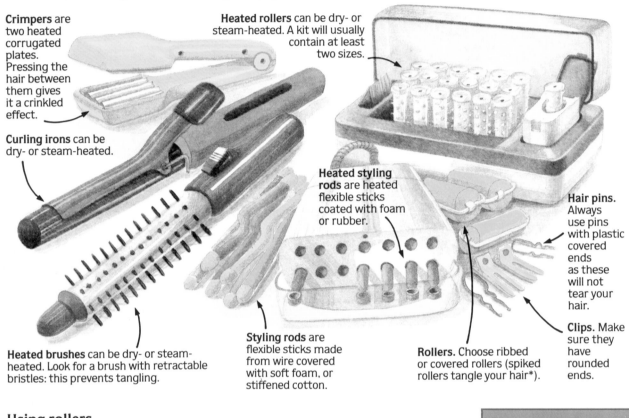

Crimpers are two heated corrugated plates. Pressing the hair between them gives it a crinkled effect.

Curling irons can be dry- or steam-heated.

Heated rollers can be dry- or steam-heated. A kit will usually contain at least two sizes.

Heated styling rods are heated flexible sticks coated with foam or rubber.

Hair pins. Always use pins with plastic covered ends as these will not tear your hair.

Clips. Make sure they have rounded ends.

Heated brushes can be dry- or steam-heated. Look for a brush with retractable bristles: this prevents tangling.

Styling rods are flexible sticks made from wire covered with soft foam, or stiffened cotton.

Rollers. Choose ribbed or covered rollers (spiked rollers tangle your hair*).

Using rollers

You can create curls by setting your hair on rollers. Cold rollers should be used on damp, towel-dried hair. Heated rollers should be used on dry hair. The technique is the same whether you use hot or cold rollers. You can see what to do below.

Starting at the front of your crown (see page 154) hold a small section of hair upwards. Wind it neatly around a roller, as shown. Then roll it down on to your head and secure it with a grip.

Repeat until the top of the head is done. For the back and sides, hold each section of hair slightly away from your head and wind the rollers towards your scalp from underneath. Secure as before.

Now leave your hair to dry. To test it, carefully unwind a roller from the thickest part of your hair. If the hair is dry, carefully remove the rest of the rollers and gently comb your hair through.

Dos and don'ts with rollers

★ Do tuck tissue paper around the ends of your hair if it is short or cut in a layered or graduated style. This makes the hair easier to roll and ensures that it lies flat giving a smooth finish.

★ Don't remove rollers before your hair is completely dry. If you do, your hair may go frizzy rather than curly.

★ Don't try to roll too much hair on to each roller or you will find that the roller falls out of your hair.

* If you have spiked rollers don't throw them away; snip off the spikes and file the stumps smooth with an emery board.

Using styling rods

You can use styling rods to make ringlets, waves or curls. Use cold rods on towel-dried hair, or heated rods on clean, dry or slightly damp hair.

Take a small section of hair and lightly twist it between your thumb and forefinger along its full length.

Wind the tress around a styling rod, and secure the ends*. Repeat until you have curled all your hair.

Leave cold rods in overnight if possible. Heated rods can be removed after about 10-15 minutes.

Using curling irons and brushes

Curling irons and brushes create instant curls and waves on dry hair. They are quick and easy to use. The technique is the same for both brushes and curling irons.

Starting underneath, take a tress and clip the rest of the hair out of your way. Grip the end of the tress in the brush or iron.

Wind the tress around the brush or iron towards your scalp. Hold for a few seconds then release carefully.

Repeat until all the hair is curled. Leave the hair to cool before brushing through, otherwise it will go limp and flat.

Using crimpers

Crimpers produce a temporary crinkled effect on dry hair**. They are quick and easy to use and the result will last until your next shampoo.

Separate a lower layer of hair. Working from the roots down, grip sections of hair in the crimpers, hold, then release.

Separate the next layer of hair and crimp it in the same way. Work your way around your head, until all the hair is crinkly.

Allow your hair time to cool. Then run your fingers through it gently to merge the sections of hair together and give it body.

Occasional curling

If you only want to curl your hair once in a while, you need not buy expensive heated appliances. You can achieve a similar effect by using a radial brush (see page 152) and your hairdryer.

1. Wind a small section of hair tightly around a small radial brush.

2. Dry the section with a hairdryer.

3. Gently remove the brush without unwinding the curl, and secure it against your head with a grip.

4. Repeat until all your hair has been curled. Leave for half an hour.

5. Remove the grips and loosen the curls with your fingers.

Dos and don'ts with heated appliances

★ Do use a conditioner or styling mousse to protect your hair.

★ Do invest in steam-heated appliances if you often use rollers, curling irons or brushes, as these are unlikely to damage your hair.

★ Do make sure that you unplug them immediately after use.

★ Don't use them as part of your daily styling routine as they dry and damage your hair.

★ Don't leave them in your hair for longer than necessary, as you may scorch and damage your hair.

★ Don't use electrical appliances in the bathroom or near water.

---

*Different styling rods are secured in different ways. Check the packet for instructions.
**You can achieve a similar effect by plaiting your hair when wet and leaving it to dry overnight.

Professional perming methods

With modern perming techniques you can achieve a wide range of textures, from a light, bouncy wave to a mass of curls. The look of a perm depends on the size and pattern of perming rods used and on the style in which the hair is cut. Below you can see how a basic perm is done. On the opposite page there are some examples of effects that can be achieved by varying the technique.

Tools of the trade

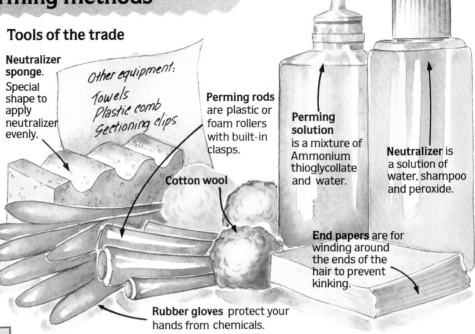

Neutralizer sponge. Special shape to apply neutralizer evenly.

Other equipment:
Towels
Plastic comb
Sectioning clips

Perming rods are plastic or foam rollers with built-in clasps.

Cotton wool

Perming solution is a mixture of Ammonium thioglycollate and water.

Neutralizer is a solution of water, shampoo and peroxide.

End papers are for winding around the ends of the hair to prevent kinking.

Rubber gloves protect your hands from chemicals.

How perming works

A perm breaks down the chemical bonds between the molecules in the hair shaft and then reconnects them in a different pattern.

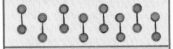

Straight hair with molecules bonded in a fixed pattern.

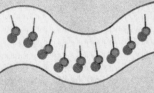

1. Hair is wound on to perming rods and perming solution is applied. It enters the cortex and breaks up the bonds between the molecules.

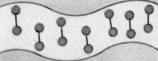

2. When neutralizer is added, the molecules reconnect, setting the hair in a curly pattern.

Perming technique*

1. Wash and towel-dry the hair. Comb out a small section of hair from the back of the crown and clip the rest out of your way. Fold a paper around the ends of the hair, as shown.

2. Place a perming rod underneath the paper and start to roll it up, gently but firmly, as shown. Continue until it rests comfortably on the scalp, then close the clasp.

3. Continue in the same way down the back of the head. Then move on to the sides and the front. Vary the size of the rods according to the texture you want to achieve.

4. Apply perming solution evenly all over the head, using the special applicator, leave on for the *exact* amount of time recommended by the manufacturer.

5. Rinse off the perming solution**. Using the sponge, dab on neutralizer in the same order as for the perming solution. Leave it on for the recommended amount of time.

6. Remove the rods and papers, then dab more neutralizer on the ends of the hair. Leave for a few more minutes. Rinse well. Finally, cut and style the hair as usual.

*Remember, you should only perm hair under the supervision of an experienced instructor.
** To shield the client's eyes, put a roll of cotton wool around her hairline while you do this.

Adapting the basic perm

Body perm. This is a soft, loose perm produced using large perming rods. This gives the hair height and volume, without making it very curly. A disadvantage of this perm is that it will start to drop out after seven or eight weeks.

Corkscrew perm. The hair is wound on to corkscrew-shaped perming rods. Alternatively, the hair can be wound in a spiral around the length of normal perming rods, and angled vertically on the head. The finished look is a mass of ringlets.

Angle perm. Instead of using perming rods, the hair is wound on to flat, plastic rectangles. Many salons use old colorant tubes split, cleaned and flattened. This produces angular kinks which give an unusual tousled effect.

Root perm. For this perm, only the roots of the hair are permed. The hair is divided into sections, and the ends wrapped tightly in pieces of plastic wrap to protect them from the solution. The resulting height and fullness create a dramatic effect.

Weave perm. A tail comb is woven in and out of sections of hair, separating a few strands from each. These strands are permed, and the rest left straight.
   This produces random curls which give the resulting style added body and an unusual texture.

Pin curl perm. The hair is divided into small sections. One section is wound around a finger. The hair is then released, and the curl clipped flat against the head. This is repeated until the head is covered in curls. Finally, a perm is applied. The result is soft, natural-looking waves.

Dos and don'ts when perming

★ Do choose a perm which is pH balanced (see page 170).

★ Do test the client's skin first (see page 162).

★ Don't perm hair more than once every four months.

★ Don't perm streaked hair, as the perm won't work evenly.

★ Don't perm hair which is out of condition.

Straightening hair

Straightening curly hair is far more risky than perming straight hair. This is because the process stretches the hair shaft, and unless it is done by an experienced professional, the hair could break off. This is the safest method:

1. Apply perming solution to the hair, avoiding the roots. Leave on for 10-15 minutes. Then divide the hair into four equal sections.

2. Starting with the back left-hand section, comb out a tress about 5mm wide. Put on more perming solution. Then coat it in petroleum jelly (to keep it straight while solution takes effect). Comb it straight again.

3. Continue in the same way until you have finished the section. then do the same with the remaining three sections. Leave for a further 10-15 minutes.

4. Apply neutralizer, as for a perm. Leave on for around 10 minutes*. Rinse, shampoo and condition the hair, keeping it as straight as possible throughout. Then style it in the usual way.

*Check the packet for guidelines.

Careers in hairdressing

There is a wide variety of exciting career opportunities within the world of hairdressing. These range from salon work or teaching to modelling or session styling.

For some careers, professional qualifications are essential: for others, experience and enthusiasm count for more. Here you can find out about some of the jobs within the hairdressing industry.

Salon hairdresser

Description: cutting clients' hair within a salon or barber's shop.

Qualifications: apprenticeship and/or formal qualifications (see pages 150-151).

Personal qualities: a good eye for detail and a sense of line and form. The ability to get on well with people and communicate your ideas clearly is also essential. Private schools also look for a good basic education.

Getting started: enrol at a college, reputable private school or academy. Alternatively, enquire about apprenticeships on leaving school (your school's career advisor should be able to help you).

Salon manager

Description: responsible for all aspects of running a salon, from making sure it is profitable to training and supervising staff.

Qualifications: none essential, but you are unlikely to succeed without some years' experience of working in a salon. A business management course is useful.

Personal qualities: business sense, good communication skills, confidence, the ability to motivate and handle staff and generate team spirit.

Getting started: work in a salon and watch the day-to-day running of it. Apply for courses in business and salon management.

Teacher

Description: teaching students of hairdressing at a college or within a private hairdressing school or academy.

Qualifications: good formal qualifications (see page 151) and experience in the hairdressing industry. You will also need a teaching diploma if working in a college.

Personal qualities: a love of hairdressing and an awareness of its trends. Enthusiasm, patience and the ability to communicate.

Getting started: build up qualifications and experience. Learn teaching skills by watching the ways others teach you.

Session stylist

Description: Styling models' hair for photographic sessions or fashion shows and demonstrations.

Qualifications: none essential, but most stylists move from salon work into session styling.

Personal qualities: good fashion sense, imagination, an eye for detail, energy, diplomacy and an ability to communicate your ideas.

Getting started: build up a portfolio (a file) of photographs of hair you have styled. You may get a chance to do this by working as an assistant to an established stylist or photographer. There are also photographic courses available which will give you a good insight into the field of hairdressing for photography.

Coloring/perming technician

Description: developing new ideas and techniques in coloring and/or perming for a large salon. Creating original looks for fashion shows and demonstrations.

Qualifications: good basic education, a formal hairdressing qualification and additional coloring and/or perming qualifications.

Personal qualities: a good understanding of scientific theory, strong color sense, artistic flair and an ability to respond quickly and imaginatively to new trends.

Getting started: train as a hairdresser. Then take specific and advanced courses in coloring and/or perming whenever possible. Acquire experience within the salon.

Demonstrator

Description: working for a large hair products company demonstrating and selling their new ranges to various clients.

Qualifications: should be a competent hairdresser who can perform well in public.

Personal qualities: a lively and outgoing personality as you will be dealing with a lot of different people. Enthusiasm and a liking for being on the move as the work also involves a lot of travelling.

Getting started: a basic hairdressing qualification (see pages 150-151) and some practical hairdressing experience is usually required by companies recruiting hair product demonstrators.

Hairdressing for television, film and theatre*

Description: styling hair for actors or television presenters. You will often work from drawings or be required to create styles from specific periods in history.

Qualifications: a good basic education. Proven ability in history and art is helpful, and sometimes essential in television. Make-up skills are often required for television.

Personal qualities: accuracy and attention to detail, tact when dealing with people, a liking for travel, stamina and adaptability as jobs may come up at very short notice and at different locations.

Getting started: some television companies train their own hairdressing and make-up staff, so apply directly to them. For film and theatre, first get a formal qualification (see pages 150-151) before applying to companies.

Public relations and marketing consultant

Description: providing publicity and up-to-date information about hairdressers, hair product manufacturers and retailers to the press and potential customers.

Qualifications: none essential, however many companies do insist on a good basic education. Some business studies courses include public relations and marketing as an additional option.

Personal qualities: business sense, good communication skills, tact and initiative.

Getting started: apply for courses in public relations and marketing or business study courses which offer these as a part of training. Alternatively, apply for any kind of job within a marketing or public relations company in order to gain experience. Some companies are also willing to recruit experienced professional hairdressers.

Modelling

Description: Modelling hairstyles and clothes for shows or photographs. It is very unusual to specialise only in modelling hairstyles.

Qualifications: none. There are modelling courses available, however unless you have the looks they are a waste of time.

Personal qualities: Healthy hair and good looks. A model also needs patience, good humour, energy and the ability to communicate.

Boys must be at least 1.78m tall, with a medium build, good looks and hair. They must start their career between the ages of 16 and 22.

Girls must be between 1.73m and 1.78m tall and take size 10** or 12** clothes. Good looks, clear skin and well-kept hair are essential. Girls must start their career between the ages of 16 and 20.

Getting started: Most regular models are chosen through agencies. Send a full length photograph and a close-up head and shoulder shot of yourself to a number of reputable agencies. Write your name, age, height and size on the back and enclose a stamped self-addressed envelope. To gain some experience you could enquire about modelling at a local hairdressing school or salon for their demonstrations or shows.

Ship's hairdresser

Description: working on board a cruise liner as the resident hairdresser.

Qualifications: good formal qualifications (see page 151). you will also need to have experience in related fields such as make-up, hair-removal and manicuring.

Personal qualities: the ability to adapt to long periods at sea, self-reliance, good communication skills, enthusiasm and patience.

Getting started: build up hairdressing and beautician experience (for example, you can apply for additional beauty courses whilst working within a salon). Then apply direct to the major cruise companies.

Wigmaker

Description: making wigs for private clients or for television, theatre or film productions.

Qualifications: a formal qualification in hairdressing and/or wigmaking. Many employers also insist that you carry out further training within the company.

Personal qualities: good manual skills, co-ordination, dedication and patience.

Getting started: start with a basic formal qualification, then apply to wig-making companies. Some television companies also employ wig-makers, however, you will need to have gained some experience before you apply to them for work.

Warning

There are an infinite number of modelling courses on offer, all of which charge a fee. Some are of a high standard, and offer good value for money. Others are overpriced and have little to offer.

Always shop around before committing yourself, and check that it is recognized by your local education authority. If possible, ask advice from someone who has already completed the course.

You will need union recognition to work in these areas.
** *European size 38, US size 8; European size 40, US size 10.*

Hair charts

Over the next five pages you will find charts telling you, at a glance, everything you need to know about hair care and styling products (such as shampoos and mousses), hair colorants, and styling equipment (such as crimpers and diffusers). There is also information on common hair problems, their causes and how to treat them.

Shampoo	Properties	Comments
For greasy hair	Contains a high proportion of detergent which strips the scalp of excess grease.	Large amounts or over-use can over-dry your scalp, causing it to flake.
For normal hair	Contains an average proportion of detergent. Cleans your hair without affecting the natural flow of oil.	The milder the better - look for products that are pH balanced (see right).
For dry hair	Contains a lower proportion of detergent - has added moisturiser. This prevents drying of the scalp and hair shaft.	Look for one with a protein or oil-enriched moisturiser.
Mild or frequent-wash	Very mild formula. Gentle on the scalp.	Recommended for all hair types. Often better for your hair than specially formulated shampoos.
Herbal	Contains extracts of various herbs and plants.	Available for all hair types – there are specific herbs for different hair conditions.
Henna	Conditions your hair and strengthens its natural color.	Continuous use may eventually dull your hair.
Colorfast	Contains little detergent. Similar to mild or frequent-wash shampoos. Prevents dyed hair from fading.	Not very effective on greasy hair.
Anti-dandruff	Contains the chemicals zinc pyrithione and selenium sulphide to slow down cell division in the scalp.	Over-use dries and dulls your hair. Alternate with your usual shampoo.
Insecticidal	Contains the chemicals malathion or carbaryl. These kill head lice.	Very harsh. Use conditioner after each treatment. You can also buy special combs which remove lice eggs.
Dry	Powder made with talcum powder or cornstarch. Absorbs oil and dirt when brushed through hair.	Takes time to remove all traces of powder. Over-use can dull your hair.
Medicated	Contains antiseptic to kill bacteria on the scalp.	Not effective on dandruff.
Silicone-based	Contains in-built conditioner.	More expensive, but saves buying conditioner.

What is a pH factor?

You may have noticed that some shampoos state their pH factor. A pH factor indicates the concentration of hydrogen in a solution. This tells you whether a substance is alkaline or acid based, as the more hydrogen there is in a substance the more alkaline it is.

The pH scale

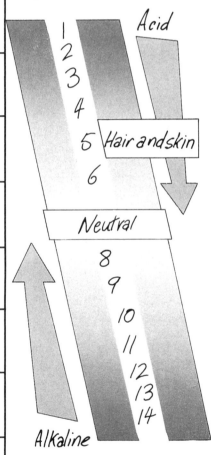

Your skin and hair have an acid content (a pH balance of 4.5-5.5). You should therefore look for products that have a similar acid balance (ideally a pH balance of 5) as these are better for your hair.

Conditioner	Properties	How to apply	Comments
Conditioning rinse	Light protein-enriched liquid that penetrates the hair shaft and strengthens it.	Leave it on your hair for about 2-3 minutes before rinsing.	Rinses away easily. Especially good for greasy hair.
Oil or cream-based balsams	Coats the hair shaft in a thin film of wax or oil, making it shiny and easy to manage.	Can be washed out immediately.	Particularly effective on thick, dry hair.
Henna wax	A thick, clear wax which leaves hair shiny and manageable.	Mix with hot water and leave on dry hair for 30 minutes.	Effective on all hair types.
Hot oil	Olive or almond oil coats the hair shaft, repairing damaged cuticles.	Warm the oil and massage into hair. Leave for as long as possible.	Particularly good for dry or damaged hair.

Hair colorant	Types available	How it works	How to apply	Durability	Comments
Temporary	Wash-in/wash-out shampoos, gels, mousses, crayons, sprays, brush-on paints, cream	Coats the hair shaft with a fine film of color.	Apply on clean, damp hair and leave to dry.	Washes out after one shampoo, or a little longer if hair is porous*.	Safe to use at home. Temporary colors do not color grey hair.
Semi-permanent	Coloring conditioner, shampoos, mousses, creams, liquids	Penetrates and colors the cuticle.	Apply on clean damp hair. Leave, for 10-20 minutes then rinse away.	4-6 weeks	Leaves hair shiny and bouncy. Will not lighten hair. Partially effective on grey hair. Over-use can dull hair.
Permanent	Liquid or cream and separate container of hydrogen peroxide (liquid chemical)	Penetrates and changes the natural color in the cortex.	Mix together the two components then apply to dry hair.	Grows out. Roots need re-touching every 4 weeks.	Good for grey hair. Too risky to try at home: should be done professionally. Dries the hair.
Bleach	Powder, paste, oil, liquid or cream; plus container of hydrogen peroxide	Penetrates the cortex and removes color from hair.	Mix together the two components and apply on dry hair.	Grows out. Roots need re-touching every 4 weeks.	Colors hair blond only. Must be done professionally.
Lighteners	Rinses or sprays	Acts in the same way as bleach (see above). Contains peroxide.	Apply on dry or damp hair. Many use the sun or heat to activate them.	Grows out. Roots need re-touching every 4 weeks.	Combination of peroxide and sunlight or heat can damage hair.
Metallic	Lotion or rinse	Contains lead or silver salts that slowly change color after several applications.	Apply on dry hair.	Grows out. Roots must be re-touched every 4 weeks.	Deposits left by the salts can damage your hair, leaving it dry and brittle.
Vegetable (Henna)	Powder	Penetrates and stains the cuticle and some of the cortex.	Mix with warm water to form paste. Then apply to damp hair.	Fades gradually.	Safe to apply at home, but very messy. May dull hair if used too often.

*This means that the hair shaft can be easily penetrated.

Styling products	Form	How to apply	Uses	Comments
Gel	Transparent jelly. Comes in jars, tubs and tubes.	Apply to the roots first and spread through dry or damp hair. Style with fingertips.	Keeps hair in position. Wet-look gel moulds hair close to the head and keeps it firmly in position.	Messy to apply. Invisible when dry (unless wet-look). If your hair is fine, use gel only on the roots.
Mousse	Comes in a pump dispenser. Has the consistency of shaving foam.	Apply to the roots of damp hair. Comb through evenly.	Holds style in place and gives it body.	Particularly effective on curly or wavy hair. Conditioning mousses are best.
Glaze	Comes as a gel in tubes.	Apply to towel-dried hair then style as normal.	Keeps hair firmly in place. Dries hard and adds shine and body to hair.	Particularly good for slicking back unruly hair. Hair needs to be styled carefully as once dry, glaze holds firm.
Grease	Comes in tubs and jars.	Apply on wet or dry hair. Either smooth on with hands or comb through.	Holds hair in place. Large quantities produce a slicked-back look.	Messy to apply. Leaves hair sticky to touch. Good for imitating fifties styles.
Setting lotion	Colorless liquid. Comes in a bottle.	Sprinkle on to towel-dried hair. Comb through and style as normal.	Adds body and keeps hair in place when dry. Use with rollers, or when a firm hold is required.	Particularly good for fine hair. Can be rather messy to apply. Leaves hair a little hard to the touch.
Blow drying lotion	Colorless liquid. Comes in a bottle.	Sprinkle on to hair before blow drying.	Similar to a setting lotion, but gives hair a softer look and feel.	Particularly good for straight, sleek cuts. Many contain a chemical which protects hair from heat.
Hairspray	Fine, quick-drying varnish which comes in an aerosol or pump dispenser.	Spray on to styled hair, from a distance of at least 20cm.	Holds finished style in place.	Use sparingly. Brushes out. Dries hair if left in too long.
Finishing spray	Light oil. Comes in aerosol or pump dispensers.	Spray on to styled hair.	Makes hair look healthy and shiny.	Particularly effective on sleek styles and slick-backed looks.
Hair gloss	Gel or oil-based. Comes in jars and tubs.	Smooth evenly through damp hair.	Keeps styled hair in place and makes it look shiny.	Gel-based gloss provides a stronger hold. Oil-based gloss is particularly good for making Afro hair shiny.
Moisturiser	Comes as cream in jars and tubs or sprays in aerosols or pump dispensers.	Apply to hair before styling.	Makes hair soft and shiny and helps loosen any tangles.	Particularly useful for conditioning Afro hair.

172

Styling equipment	Description	Uses	What to look for	Comments
Brush	Available in different types such as vent, styling and radial (see page 152).	For brushing and styling dry hair only.	Look for natural or synthetic bristles with rounded ends.	Wash regularly. Check bristles by pressing them into your palm: if they hurt they are too sharp.
Comb	Available with close or wide-set teeth (or both combined).	For styling and untangling wet or dry hair.	Choose wide-toothed synthetic combs with rounded ends.	Wash regularly in shampoo and warm water. Never use metal combs as they tear the hair.
Hairdryer	Hand-held, electrically-powered drying tool.	For blow drying hair.	Look for one with several temperature settings and a nozzle attachment to diffuse the heat.	Alway use on a low temperature setting, and hold at least 10cm from the hair.
Rollers	Small plastic or foam cylinders, held in place by clips.	For curling and perming hair.	Choose ribbed or fabric covered rollers rather than the spiky sort.	Store them in a clean bag or box.
Styling rods	Flexible foam, rubber or fabric-covered wires.	For curling and perming hair.	Check the ones you buy are very bendy. Choose good quality fabric ones if you are leaving them in overnight.	Create a softer look than rollers.
Heated rollers	Rollers which are electrically or steam-heated in a special container before use.	For curling hair quickly.	Look for rollers with a smooth surface. Choose steam-heated ones if you intend to use them often.	Over-use may make hair dry, especially at the ends.
Heated styling rods	Styling rods which are electrically-heated before use in a special container.	For curling hair quickly.	Choose very flexible ones covered in good quality foam or rubber.	Better for your hair than conventional heated rollers as you do not need clips to secure them.
Crimpers	Two thermostatically-controlled plates with crinkly surfaces, between which the hair is pressed.	Makes hair crinkly.	Choose crimpers that are lightweight and easy to handle.	Use on conditoned hair. Do not brush crimped hair.
Straighteners	Two thermostatically-controlled flat plates between which the hair is pressed.	Straighten curly or wavy hair.	Choose straighteners which are lightweight and easy to handle.	Do not use too often. Do not brush your hair once it has been straightened.
Curling irons	Hand-held, cylindrical hinged clamp which is electrically or steam-heated.	For curling hair quickly.	Choose steam-heated irons, as they are better for your hair.	Do not use too often. Start with the irons right at the ends of your hair, to avoid kinks.
Heated brush	Electrically or steam-heated radial brush.	For curling hair quickly.	Look for retractable bristles. These prevent the hair from tangling when the brush is removed.	Do not use too often. Once curled, it is best to style the hair with your fingers or a comb.

Styling equipment	Description	Uses	What to look for	Comments
Scissors	Hairdressing scissors are specially designed for the purpose (see page 152).	For cutting hair.	Choose very sharp, lightweight ones. Short blades will give you more control.	It is worth spending the money to get really good quality scissors.
Diffuser	Large round nozzle attachment for hairdryer which spreads air-flow more widely.	Dries hair gently and steadily without blowing it around.	Make sure you buy one which fits your make and size of dryer.	Good for styling curly or wavy hair. Can only be bought through trade outlets.
Clippers	Small hand-held electrically operated razor.	Cuts hair very close to the head.	Look for lightweight clippers with sharp blades.	Only use clippers if you are professionally qualified. Take care not to nip the skin.

Hair problem	Symptoms	Causes	Solutions
Dandruff	Itchy scalp, white flakes in hair and dropping onto shoulders.	The cells of the skin multiply too quickly and the dead cells build up and flake off. May be stress-related.	Can be controlled, but not cured. Alternate between your normal shampoo and an anti-dandruff shampoo. Resist the temptation to scratch your scalp.
Split ends (Fragilitas crinium)	Hair has dull, frizzy appearance as small ends stick out.	The end of the hair shaft splits in two because the hair has worn out, or is damaged by heated appliances, chemicals or harsh brushing.	Have hair trimmed regularly.
Hair breaking	Hair feels brittle and is dull in appearance. Tends to break off in clumps while brushing and combing.	Usually self-inflicted, through using harsh chemicals, heated appliances, brushing too vigorously, pulling hair into tight styles or using rubber bands.	Use fabric-covered bands to tie hair up. Avoid harsh treatments and heated appliances. Never rub or tug hair.
Static	When brushed, hair stands out and crackles. Difficult to style and looks dull.	Cuticles of each hair may have been damaged so that they are rough instead of smooth. Rough or dry hairs rub against each other and produce static when brushed.	Use a light conditioner which smooths the cuticle and neutralizes the electrical charge.
Head lice	Very itchy scalp. Examining the scalp under a good light reveals lice and white egg sacks.	Contact with another afflicted person.*	Use an insecticidal shampoo prescribed by your doctor and follow the instructions carefully. Ask all members of your family to use it too, as lice spread easily.
Grey hair	Hair appears grey in color (individual hairs are in fact white – it is the mixture of white and natural color that gives an illusion of grey).	Grey hair has no color pigment in the cortex (see page 131). It can be caused by shock, illness, stress or ageing.	Disguise grey hair by coloring it to match the rest of your hair.

Lice breed in clean hair. Anyone can become infected, so there is no need to feel embarrassed.

Going further

If you would like to find out about any aspect of hairdressing, the books and selected contact addresses listed below will give you a good starting point.

Book list

General

African Hairstyles: Styles of Yesterday and Today
Esi Sagay
Heinemann

An Illustrated Dictionary of Hairdressing and Wigmaking
James Stevens Fox
Batsford

Fashions in Hair: The First Five Thousand Years
Richard Carson
Peter Owen
(distributed in the US & Canada by Dufour Editions Inc.)

The Miriam Stoppard Health & Beauty Book
Dorling Kindersley
(not available in the US or Canada)

Hair Matters
Joshua & Daniel Galvin
MacMillan
(not available in the US or Canada)

Hair Care: Deborah McCormick
The Body Shop Book
MacDonald

Vogue Guide to Hair Care
Felicity Clark
Penguin

Career

Becoming a Hairdresser
Pauline Wheatley
Batsford

Coloring: a salon handbook
Lesley Hatton
Blackwell
(distributed in the US by BSP Inc. and in Canada by OUP)

Science for Hairdressing Students
(3rd edition)
Lee & Inglis
Pergamon Press

Working in Hairdressing
Marina Thaine & Robert Griffin
Batsford

Cutting Hair the Vidal Sassoon Way
(2nd edition)
William Heinemann

Cutting and Styling: A Salon Handbook
Hatton & Hatton
Collins
(distributed in the US by BSP Inc. and in Canada by OUP)

Hygiene: A Salon Handbook
Philip Hatton
Blackwell
(distributed in the US by BSP Inc. and in Canada by OUP)

Mastering Hairdressing
Leo Palladino
MacMillan Masters Series
(not available in the US or Canada)

Perming & Straightening: A Salon Handbook
Hatton & Hatton
Blackwell
(distributed in the US by BSP Inc. and in Canada by OUP)

Useful addresses

UK

British Association of Professional Hairdresser Employers
1a Barbon Close
Great Ormond Street
London WC1 3JX

City and Guilds of London Institute
46 Britannia Street
London WC1X 9RG

Hairdressing Training Board
Silver House Silver Street
Doncaster DN1 1HL

The Guild of Hairdressers
24 Woodbridge Road
Guildford
Surrey GU1 1DY

The Hairdressing Council
12 David House
45 High Street
South Norwood
London SE25 6HJ

Vidal Sassoon School of Hairdressing
56-58 Davies Mews
London
W1Y 1AS

Vidal Sassoon Education Centre
19-21 King Street
Manchester

Australia

Hairdressing and Beauty Industry Association
1202 Toorak Road
Hartwell Victoria
Australia 3125

New Zealand

New Zealand Council of Ladies Hairdressing Associations
PO Box 28-322
Auckland 5

US

National Association of Cosmetologists
3510 Olive Street
St Louis
Mo 63103

Vidal Sassoon Academy & School of Cosmetology
1222 Santa Monica Mall
California 90401

Canada

National Canadian Hairdressers & Cosmetologists Association Incorporated
1982 Islington Avenue
Weston
Ontario M9P 3N5

Vidal Sassoon Educational Center
37 Avenue Road
Toronto M5R 2G3

Index

Acknowledgements

For part one

Cover photographs, top left: Yves Saint Laurent (photographer Niall McInerney), top right: Emanuel Ungaro (photographer Niall McInerney): **page 3**, centre left: Betty Jackson (photographer Niall McInerney), bottom left: courtesy of Mr Marc Massin; **page 4,** courtesy of British Courtelle Awards; **page 6,** bottom left: courtesy of Chanel, bottom right: courtesy of Illustrated London News Picture Library; **page 7,** courtesy of Dior: **page 8,** courtesy of Mary Quant; **page 9,** Rei Kawakubo for Comme des Garçons (photographer Peter Lindbergh) **page 17,** courtesy of London College of fashion (photographer David Whittington-Jones); **page 20,** Milan: Gianfranco Ferre (photographer Niall McInerney), Paris: Karl Lagerfeld (photographer Niall McInerney); **page 21,** London: courtesy of Katherine Hamnett, New York: Donna Karan (photographer Pierre Sherman), Tokyo: Issey Miyake (photographer Niall McInerney); **page 24,** top: Giorgio Armani (photographer Aldo Fallai), centre: Pierre Balmain, courtesy of Pierre Balmain et Cie, bottom: courtesy of Chanel; **page 25,** top: design drawing by Marc Bohan for Dior, centre: courtesy of Gianfranco Ferre, bottom: Bill Gibb (photographer John Adriaan); **page 26,** top: Betty Jackson (photographer Niall McInerney), centre left: Norma Kamali (photographer Niall McInerney), centre right: Donna Karan (photographer Pierre Sherman), bottom: Rei Kawakubo for Comme des Garçons (photographer Steven Meisle); **page 27,** top: Ralph Lauren (photographer Bruce Weber), centre: Claude Montana (photographer Niall McInerney), bottom: Jean Muir (photographer Michael Barrett); **page 28,** top left: Dinny Hall for Bruce Oldfield (photographer John Carter), top right: courtesy of House of Patou, centre left: courtesy of Mary Quant*, centre right: Jill Green for Zandra Rhodes (photographer Robyn Beeche), bottom: Yves Saint Laurent (photographer Niall McInerney), centre left and right: courtesy of Mr Marc Massin; **page 29,** top: Gianni Versace (photographer Niall McInerney), centre left and right: courtesy of Mr Marc Massin, bottom: Yohji Yamamoto (photograher Niall McInerney); **page 30,** left: copyright Sevenarts Ltd, courtesy of Haper's Bazaar (British edition), right: courtesy of Mr Marc Massin.

For part two

Photographer **Simon Bottomley**
Session co-ordinator **Saskia Sarginson**
Stylist **Sara Sarre**
Make-up and hair **Louise Constad**

Hair, pages 79, 81, 82-83, 93 **Tony Collins** for Joshua Galvin
Models **Mickey** at Synchro, **Akure** at Look, **Emma Campbell** and **Louise Kelly** at Select

The following organizations kindly gave permission to reproduce the photographs on these pages:

page 74 left, Elle/Transworld
page 74 right and centre, and page 75 right, Jacinte/Transworld
page 75 left, Fashion Fair
page 75 centre, Seventeen at Boots

The following companies kindly contributed clothes and accessories for the photographs:

Liberty, Goldie, Fenwicks, Corocraft, Katherine Glazier and Extras (both at Hyper Hyper), Alexis Lahellec, Oui, Hyper Hyper, Molton Brown, The Yarn Store, Neal Street East. All room sets from Habitat.

For part three

Photographer **Simon Bottomley**
Stylist **Carol Garbera**
Make-up **Wendy Saad** at Joy Goodman
Hair **Carlo Braida** at Shumi
Model **Louise Kelly** at Select

For part four

Photographers: Robyn Beeche, Tim Bret-Day, Peter Brown, Marc Bucklow, Peter Calvin, Roger Eaton, Karen Elmers, Martin Evening, Melissa Halstead, Christian Hartman, Stevie Hughes, Mark Lewis, James Martin, Jean Pierre Masclet, Eamonn J McCabe, Al McDonald, Stephen Murphy, Mike Owen, Malcolm Pasley, Jonathan Rea, David Schienmann.

Agencies: Askews, Bookings, Count Eight, Edit, Folio, Freddies, Gavins, Laraine Ashton, Look, Marco Rasala, Models One Elite, Models One Men, Nevs, Premier, Review, Select, Strorm, Synchro, Take Two, Unique, Wills Dells, Ziggy.

First published in 1988 by Usborne Publishing Ltd, 20 Garrick Street, London WC2E 9BJ, England. Coyright © 1988 Usborne Publishing.

Printed in Belgium   American edition 1989.

For part four (Hair and Hairstyling):
Haircare Limited is the sole and exclusive licensee of Richardson-Vicks Inc and Proctor & Gamble Ltd within the United Kingdom of Great Britain and all rights are hereby reserved.

* Whilst every effort was made to trace the photographer of these designs, his/her identity was still unknown at the time of going to press.